"**What is the meaning of this, I wonder?**"

Her voice was usually quiet, yet now it had a sharp ring to it like thunder.

AN ARCHDEMON'S DILEMMA: HOW TO LOVE YOUR ELF BRIDE

The time to regain
your original bodies has come!
Onward to the ocean metropolis!

"Hello, Silver-Eyed King."

The one standing before him was a small girl.

"What do you want?"

It would have been fine to ignore her, but Zagan stopped because she was the first person he'd managed to meet in the area.

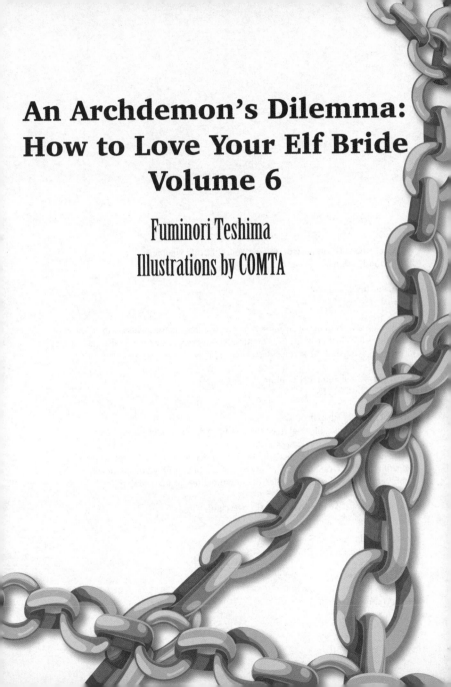

An Archdemon's Dilemma: How to Love Your Elf Bride Volume 6

Fuminori Teshima

Illustrations by COMTA

An Archdemon's Dilemma: How to Love Your Elf Bride Volume 6
by Fuminori Teshima

Translated by Hikoki
Edited by DxS

Copyright © 2018 Fuminori Teshima
Illustrations by COMTA

First published in Japan in 2018
Publication rights for this English edition arranged through Hobby Japan, Tokyo.

Find more books like this one at www.j-novel.club!

President and Publisher: Samuel Pinansky
Managing Editor: Aimee Zink

ISBN: 978-1-7183-5705-1
Printed in Korea
First Printing: July 2020
10 9 8 7 6 5 4 3 2 1

Contents

"What's the meaning of this, Chastille!?" Nephteros burst into Chastille's office and immediately began shouting. She jumped up from her chair, which made her red hair, that was tied to the left side of her head, go flying about, and the quill pen in her right hand sent droplets of ink flying through the area. Since she was in her office, she was wearing an ultramarine uniform instead of her usual Anointed Armor.

The woman facing her, Nephteros, had silver hair and golden eyes. Her dark skin and pointy ears were characteristic of dark elves, who were said to possess considerable power even among the elves. The documents that she threw down on Chastille's desk seemed to be related to the Angelic Knights' salaries.

"M-Miss Nephteros, please calm down. What happened?"

"Please wait, Lady Nephteros, I'm sure Lady Chastille had much to consider."

Behind her was Kuroka, a young girl with black hair who seemed all flustered, and a young Angelic Knight. The triangular ears atop Kuroka's head were twitching about. She was a tabaxi. Her red eyes had no light in them, and she held a long cane in her hand. She was blind.

"Eeek!? D-Did I do something wrong!?"

"Don't just go, 'did I do something wrong?' Why did you cut down the personal expenses of the Angelic Knights!?"

"W-Well, I mean, the donations have gone down, so I have to manage the funds somehow…"

"Then don't let the donations go down! Do you think these people put their lives on the line for a mere pittance!? Are you stupid!? Do you want to cause a revolt!?" Nephteros began arguing vehemently with an extremely menacing attitude, putting Chastille on the verge of tears. And as she did, the three knights who served as her subordinates cut in.

"W-Wait, please calm down, Lady Nephteros."

"Please leave it at that. We do not have any complaints regarding our current… Sorry, it's nothing."

The brawny knights were pitifully rendered silent by a single glare from Nephteros.

Is she trying to make me confess the real reason why I did this? It seemed she hadn't burst in just to reject her decision without even listening to what Chastille had to say. And so, Chastille nervously opened her mouth while twiddling her index fingers.

"My predecessor solicited quite a large sum of donations from the people. If we attempt to raise more, then the people won't even be able to live. Having said that, it would be absurd to cut down the condolence fees we send to the families of those who've died in the line of duty, so there was no other way to cut costs…"

Just a few days ago, because of the chimera Archdemon Bifrons threw into town, several Angelic Knights had perished. There were also a number of casualties several months ago, so the cost of condolence fees to their families and the cost for replacing them had put a lot of pressure on their finances. In that case, the only possible course of action was hiking up the cost of donations, but there was also a reason they couldn't do that.

I know it's wrong to feel this way, but I can't have them favor Zagan... Archdemon Zagan was a king among sorcerers. However, contrary to his villainous countenance, the trust the people had in him ran deep. That was because despite being an Archdemon, he would wander around town aimlessly, look after the people, and would even incidentally protect the weak. Quite a large amount of people in the town had been saved by him already.

Moreover, he always had his elf lover by his side... and the way they had awkwardly built up their love for one another had somehow become one of the town's famous sights. Seeing him acting the fool had made their hate for sorcerers dissipate. And since the church and sorcerers were enemies on the surface, an increase in trust toward Zagan also meant a decrease in trust toward the church, which would only make the donations worse.

Nephteros let out a sigh and picked up an unfinished document from Chastille's desk.

"In that case, stop using this stupidly expensive parchment. It takes fifty whole sheep just to make a single book out of this stuff, you know? There are also far cheaper inks out there, right?"

The parchment they used was made out of sheepskin. They could only get about six sheets' worth out of a single sheep, so even four sheets of it were equal to the wage of a regular citizen. It was far cheaper to use paper made out of plants, but since those were largely manufactured by sorcerers, it was considered more meaningful to the church to use parchment for official documents.

"No, sorry. That's something the church headquarters has decided is absolutely necessary, so I can't just substitute them for something cheaper..."

"That doesn't apply to everything, right? Besides, if you're lacking in donations, then you should be selling that parchment or thinking of other ways of making money."

"I-I doubt the people would be interested in this parchment…"

"If you just sell it as-is, then it probably won't sell. But why not write about your scriptures, or saints, or the heroic tales of Angelic Knights, and turn it into a book? Those rich collectors would probably buy them, and if you spread books around like that, then you'll be able to regain some trust, right?"

Nephteros has really thought this through, huh? Chastille had no way of refuting that idea. Something like making books and selling them had never even occurred to Chastille. That was why she honestly showed her gratitude for the idea.

"I see. Making books sounds like a great idea. I'll put it to the test right away. Thanks, Nephteros."

"H-Hmph! It's fine as long as you get it." Nephteros stated that and turned to the side as her pointy ears were dyed red right to their tips. Upon seeing her reaction, the faces of three knights who were trembling in fear loosened up. And perhaps because she was the only one unable to keep up with the conversation, Kuroka had been staring blankly at them the whole time, and after a short while, she finally smiled.

"Miss Nephteros, you were getting angry on behalf of all the Angelic Knights, right? You really are kind."

"Wh-Why do I have to worry about you lot!?" Nephteros roared. It had been about a week since Nephteros and Kuroka had taken up residence at the church. And before they knew it, the position of an official aide that Kuroka came to fill in the first place was being done by Nephteros. Since the other Angelic Knights were worried about the idea and volunteered to explain everything to her, she was already capable of managing the church's finances.

"It's nothing... I'm a freeloader, so I'll at least help out." Nephteros said that paper-thin excuse repeatedly. But even so, she often went too far with her words, and at such times, Kuroka would cut in to mediate.

"But, you were thinking of everybody in town, right Lady Chastille? I'm sure everyone will be happy about it!"

"..." Chastille covered her face, clearly embarrassed by Nephteros' caring attitude. Thanks to these girls, her burden at the church had lightened a fair bit.

The misunderstanding with Kuroka was resolved, too... That was what Chastille was most happy about. When they first met, Kuroka only thought of Chastille as a target and tried to kill her. She was a girl who, on top of being blind, had a gentle personality and seemed completely unrelated to any forms of violence, but with a sword in her hand, she became a master who could rival Chastille. She even possessed enough skill to completely overwhelm Chastille when they were in the confined environment of the office, so it wasn't all that appealing a situation to have this girl aiming for her life.

She was being led on by Archdemon Bifrons, but the biggest cause of the misunderstanding was Chastille's own misleading speech and conduct. It was to the point where she was astonished at how confusing the words she said were, and her sorcerer escort, Barbatos, roared with laughter, exclaiming, 'Now there's the usual Chastille!' Just remembering that somehow made her sad.

Huh? I feel like Barbatos has been calling me by my name lately... In the end, she wasn't all that happy about being treated like a useless crybaby, but did that mean the sorcerer with a foul personality had acknowledged her in some way? Chastille shook her head as if trying to shake away such thoughts, then looked down at the order written on the document before her.

Archangel Chastille Lillqvist. I request your attendance at the Continental Interracial Elders Conference as a representative of the church.

That was the name of the gathering which would assemble all the continent's races. *I wonder if they'll all attend?*

"Clothes… for a date?"

Nighttime. Zagan found himself at a loss for words upon being informed of something by his butler Raphael. Three days had passed since he invited Nephy on a date, but they hadn't actually gone yet. There was a large increase in the number of residents in his castle thanks to the aftermath of Bifrons' attack on Kianoides, which left them all swamped in work. Nephy herself was busy running about, dealing with all the housework in the castle.

Bifrons still manages to get in my way even after their defeat. Archdemons are really something else… It wasn't like it was all Bifrons' fault, but that was where Zagan decided to point his resentment. And with all that going on, it was decided that the date would finally occur one week later, but… Raphael had suddenly brought up the topic of clothing as if he had remembered something.

As always, Zagan had a fiendish countenance that could make a child cry on sight. His black hair, which he had previously disregarded entirely, was at least combed down and tied back, but it didn't really change much, and he wore a completely plain black robe underneath his red mantle. Zagan looked down at his own clothing in shock, then turned back to his butler.

"I can't just go in these?"

"...My liege. Think it over. Between Lady Nephy showing up to your date wearing her usual maid uniform, and Lady Nephy showing up after putting all her effort into her appearance... which would make you happier?"

"Isn't it obvious that both would make me happy!?" Zagan replied with a serious expression on his face. That was his immediate reaction. Zagan had no intentions of making Nephy wear something embarrassing, and she already looked stunning in her maid uniform. Naturally, the dress she was wearing when he first met her was also quite lovely, but that didn't really matter. It was impossible for Zagan to assign a ranking to how she looked.

"That is not what I mean... Then, are you perhaps saying that you do not care what Lady Nephy wears?" Raphael asked as he put his hand to his forehead in a troubled manner.

"No, that's a different matter altogether. Well, I certainly do wish for her to wear new clothes on our date, but... I see. So that's what you mean."

His butler certainly had a point. Zagan definitely wanted to see Nephy getting all worried about what clothes to wear for his sake... Plus, he genuinely wanted to see her dressed up as well. In that case, Nephy would surely also be happy to see Zagan wearing properly selected clothes.

But... aren't these the only clothes I possess? The reason sorcerers wore such unfashionable robes and mantles wasn't because of their whims or to create some sort of atmosphere. They were fortresses which were implanted with all forms of magic circles for defense, offense, physical reinforcement, and regeneration. It wasn't something that could be planted into the flimsy shirts or fancy trousers that nobles and commoners wore. However, that wasn't a good enough reason for Zagan to go on his date dressed like a slob.

He still had a week, so he still had time to do something to remedy the situation.

"Tell me, Raphael. What should I do? What sort of clothing would be appropriate?"

"I am also not well versed in this area. However, you may wish to start by fixing your hygiene."

"My hygiene!?"

Now that he mentioned it, Zagan realized that he wore the same clothes every day. If they got dirty or began to smell, he could deal with it using sorcery. And because he could decompose sweat and dirt in the tiniest crevices down to the last bacteria, it wasn't like he was in any way filthy. However, whether or not it was hygienic was a different issue.

"Also, a gentleman would surely at least wear a tie," Raphael added.

"A tie? I don't even own one of those," Zagan groaned. The only thing he owned that was even close was a rope used to hang people.

Surely, when the time came that Nephy and the others could live freely under the light of the sun, Zagan would have to wear normal clothes and live out a normal life. And so, his current hurdle was acquiring that first 'normal' set of clothes. A date was apparently something a normal couple did, after all.

"Then… I guess I have to go out and buy some clothes…" Zagan quietly muttered, seemingly resigning himself to his fate. Though, he was certain he would have to do it without letting any of the other sorcerers in his castle find out. Especially Gremory.

"Raphael, you understand what it is that you must do, right?" Zagan asked as he aimed a sharp gaze over to Raphael.

"A foolish question, my liege. All I need do is keep your true intentions hidden from everyone and seal the movements of those damn sorcerers, right?"

On one hand was the youngest Archdemon in history with a villainous countenance. On the other was the most dreadful ex-Archangel with an enormous scar across his face, who had a body count that neared 500. The scene of the two of them having a confidential conversation was enough to make one think they were plotting dastardly deeds. But, in truth, they were just discussing the small worry of 'what should I do to look good?' In any case, Zagan nodded in satisfaction at Raphael's response, which perfectly lined up with his own intentions.

"I see that my butler is as impressive as ever. I'll leave the castle to you."

"Understood."

All that was left was procuring clothes fit for a date. Having said that, it was a little late in the evening to head out, since it was just about time for dinner. He realized that if he wanted to head into town, it would have to be rather late in the night or during the following morning.

I don't have time for this... This may be a dangerous move... but should I count on Manuela...? Thinking back on all the times she picked clothes for the others, he knew he ran the risk of being used like a toy, but that suspicious clerk's eyes could be trusted. She would definitely pick out clothing suitable for a date... Or rather, there wasn't really any other store where he could even ask for such a thing. Zagan's name was too well known in Kianoides. If he were to order them to choose clothes for an Archdemon at their own discretion, most clerks would just cower without giving him a proper response.

It was good fortune that Raphael had pointed it out to him with a week to spare. He truly was rather useful. And right about when he was deciding on what the optimal timing would be to slip out of the castle unnoticed...

"This is all, like, a total misunderstanding, little missy! I was just, like, kind of interested in what was inside! Or, like, I thought maybe it was addressed to me!"

"What's going on...?" Zagan and Raphael knit their brows upon hearing that headache inducing scream. Shortly thereafter, the door opened along with a knock. The one who entered after that was Foll, and she was dragging Selphy along by the neck. As always, Foll had her green hair in braids running down her back, and she had dragon horns sticking out behind her ears. Her amber eyes were sparkling, and judging from the rough breath coming from her nose, she seemed to be mad about something. This young girl was a descendant of dragons, and was also Zagan's adopted daughter. She had Selphy in her left hand and an envelope in her right.

As for Selphy... Well, she was a girl with blue hair. She had quite the pretty face when silent, but right now she was letting out a waterfall of tears while begging for her life. And perhaps because it was drenched by her tears, the lower half of her body had transformed into that of a fish's tail and was wriggling about. She was a siren. And, as one might expect, her specialty was singing. However, even her crying voice was abnormally noisy.

"Can I come in?" Foll looked up at Zagan and Raphael, came to a stop, and asked that question. Apparently, she could tell that they were talking about something serious, and was asking whether she was being a nuisance.

Well, it's not like it was anything too important. I was just asking for dating advice... From the outside, there was a sense of tension in the air that made the meeting seem extremely serious and dangerous, but Zagan himself did not know that.

"Yeah. We're just about finished. You may come in."

"Here. A letter for you," Foll walked all the way up to Zagan with her baggage in tow.

"Oh. Good work... By the way, what is that?" Zagan inquired as he cast his gaze over to Selphy.

"It's totally a misunderstanding, Mister Archdemon! I wasn't, like, trying to read your letter or anything, I swear! I'm not that brave!" Selphy began appealing to him in a booming voice as tears streamed down her face.

"Then why were you opening it?" Foll asked with a glare.

"...I don't really get what's going on. Did she try to read my letter or something?"

"Yeah," Foll replied. It seemed she had caught her red-handed.

"Well, I doubt anything important would get sent to me by letter, but you still shouldn't open other people's letters without permission. If it was a letter from a sorcerer, it could've exploded the moment you opened it."

"That's not it, okay? The sender of that letter's from my home, right? So I thought, like, maybe they sent it here for me..." Selphy mumbled in a cracking voice. She had turned ghastly pale and began trembling violently upon hearing Zagan's earlier warning. She probably wasn't lying or anything. This girl was rather thoughtless on occasion, but she at least understood that she was working in a place where she could die just by Zagan's whim. However, in that case, the letter itself was rather incomprehensible.

"Why would a letter come from your home? I don't know any other sirens."

"That's why I thought it was, like, for me..." Selphy replied in a completely dispirited tone, which made Zagan shrug his shoulders.

"I understand your circumstances for now. You may release her, Foll."

"Fine."

"Whoa!" Selphy's head slammed into the marble floor as Foll abruptly let her go. After watching her tumble around the ground as she gripped her head, Zagan turned to Foll.

"Foll, you should treat animals with a bit more care. Unlike sorcerers, they're weak and may die right away," Zagan chastised her in a sympathetic tone.

"...I didn't notice. I'll be more careful next time," Foll replied. Zagan gently brushed Foll's head after she obediently apologized, which made Selphy shift her attention over to him in displeasure.

"An animal... Well, I guess it's good that you at least recognize me as a living, breathing creature..." Selphy muttered. In any case, Foll went out of her way to deliver that letter to him, so Zagan quickly traced his finger along the edge of the envelope, which was enough to open it as if a knife was passed through it. Then, the letter inside flew out. It wasn't something so grandiose that one would call it sorcery, as all he had done was use mana to sever the paper. And, as the letter settled itself in front of his eyes, Zagan knit his brows.

"The Continental Interracial Elders Conference?"

He'd never heard of it before. This continent was host to a countless number of races, including elves and all the therianthropes. Among those, races like the dragons and elves had low populations. Based on the contents of the letter, it looked to be a meeting for all the races to attend, but...

"Hm..." Raphael muttered in interest before saying, "It's a conference held for the representatives of each race. There are those among them who are practically on the verge of extinction, so it may be a conference that's supposed to help them find a way to survive, or start a cultural exchange of sorts. And whatever is decided there will be adopted by all races within the continent."

"You're quite well informed on the matter, aren't you?"

"That is because the representative for the humans is selected from among the church. I have never attended myself, but I at least know the general outline of it. This time around, someone like Chastille was most likely selected."

Sorcerers were humans who lived in the underworld. When it came to a gathering of races on the surface, it was only obvious that personnel from the church would be selected.

"We were also told to, like, run to the church if sorcerers were after us. They take money, but they do shelter the other races at least," Selphy said, adding her own input. This was something Zagan only learned about when he picked up Kuroka and Kuu on a whim the other day, but the church had a side to it that was akin to a refugee shelter. That was why the people still relied on the church despite the high cost of donations. He understood that fact, but still, Zagan let out an astonished voice.

"Did you forget that this is a sorcerer's castle?"

"Uhhh, I guess it is, huh?" Selphy mumbled those words in a dumbfounded voice. How was she such a scatterbrain?

"But this letter means they want me, a sorcerer, to attend as well. Have they gone senile? This is like a big, fat sheep inviting a hungry wolf over, isn't it?" Zagan cocked his head to the side as he asked that question.

They couldn't be thinking that a sorcerer, let alone an Archdemon, is virtuous, could they? Selphy had hinted at the idea earlier, but the reason so many species were on the verge of extinction was because of sorcerers. There were many non-human races who had inherent magical properties, so sorcerers hunted them down to use them as catalysts and sacrifices. And yet, they were inviting a sorcerer over to an important gathering. However, the only one laughing at the idea was Zagan.

"You really don't get it sometimes, Zagan," Foll said that in an unusually astonished voice.

"Huh…? Did I say something strange?" Zagan inquired. In response, Foll made a face like it would be a pain to explain it to him, and in her stead, Raphael turned to Zagan with a strained smile on his face.

"My liege. This castle houses a high elf, a dragon, a fomorian, a leonin, and recently, even a siren. It would be unreasonable for them not to be interested when there are so many races coexisting here with no conflict to speak of. There are countless endangered species out there that require protection, after all."

"Oh…" Zagan muttered. Setting aside Nephy and Foll, the others were all people who dropped in of their own accord, so he found that conclusion hard to accept. And so, he lowered his gaze back down to the letter as if trying to gloss over it, then knit his brows once more and said, "I don't really care what the other races are thinking, but this letter says I'm to go with the envoy. Did someone bring this letter to the castle? They haven't been killed, right?"

It was an envoy for a conference of all the races, so there was a very high probability that they were someone of rather high standing. In that case, they were like a sitting duck to a bunch of salivating sorcerers. Be they human or of the other races, Zagan thought nothing of someone he didn't know dying. Still, it certainly left a bad aftertaste if someone who came here specially for him was carelessly killed by his subordinates before he even got a chance to speak to them. And so, he turned to Selphy in search of answers.

"Uhhh, what's up?"

"I mean, you were carrying this letter, right? Where did you get it?"

"Huh…? It was, just, like, brought over by a carrier pigeon."

23

"A carrier pigeon?"

It's not like that carrier pigeon was the envoy or anything, right? It was unclear how many of the races were attending, so he was left confused.

"The name that's written here is Ainselph Thalasa Neptuna… a third princess from somewhere or other," Zagan read the name on the letter out loud, which made Selphy tilt her head to the side with a blank expression.

"Huh, me?" Selphy asked. And this time, it wasn't just Zagan, but everyone present who glared back at her.

"Now's not the time for such jokes," Zagan said with a sigh.

"So mean! All I did was react to my own name!" Selphy exclaimed, completely shocked by their hate-filled words and gazes.

"Your names might be similar, but it says princess here. It's someone else," Foll replied in an admonishing tone.

"But I'm, like, totally a princess!"

"Has being dragged here made you lose your mind?" Foll replied with a hint of pity in her eyes.

"Gaaah, it's true! Selphy is short for Ainselph! And Thalasa is, like, a name that can only be used by siren royalty. I totally wouldn't lie about this!" Selphy exclaimed as she was on the verge of tears, which made Raphael peer in at her face with a puzzled expression.

"Hm… Now that you mention it, I've heard that sirens with blue hair are part of a special bloodline…"

"Right? Right!? Look, aren't I, like, super elegant?"

"Not at all," Raphael replied without a moment's hesitation, rendering Selphy completely silent. Zagan found this somewhat pitiful, so he decided to at least hear her out.

"Well, for the sake of argument, if you're royalty, why were you working as a singer atop a sorcerer's boat and getting drunk in a bar because you were unemployed?"

"It's not just for the sake of argument! I'm, like, totally not lying!" Selphy roared as she stood up languidly, and because all her crying earlier had wet her face, she was wiping the tip of her nose bashfully as she said, "Well, you see, our people kind of have this rule where royal songs are, like, sacred or something, right? So, they can only be listened to by, like, a chosen few. I didn't like that, so I ran away from home. I never thought I'd end up as a servant at your castle, though!"

"So, what's with you being an envoy?" Zagan asked. Watching this girl laugh without a care in the world was starting to give him a headache.

Selphy folded her arms and racked her brain over the matter. It seemed the person in question didn't know either.

After waiting in silence for the second hand of the clock to make a full lap, Selphy finally clapped her hands together.

"Oh, maybe it's that. Like, my family's been real worried about me staying at your place, Mister Archdemon, since I sent them a letter about it. So, like, they wrote to bring you along next time around."

"Why didn't you say anything earlier?" Zagan asked.

"Ahaha, I mean, like, even I'm not shameless enough to drag you down to my place beneath the ocean, Mister Archdemon," Selphy replied. For the time being, it seemed that she was at least aware that she was shameless.

Although, I guess this timing makes sense now... The sirens knew about Zagan because of Selphy's letters, so the elders probably thought to call him over to that conference.

"I know I may not look it, but I am busy here..." Zagan said as he tossed the letter onto a table as if it was garbage. His date with Nephy was fast approaching. He only had a week left to prepare.

I also can't bring myself to keep Orias waiting much longer... Zagan's focus shifted over to his pocket, where he had left a mithril pendant, as he thought that.

Archdemon Orias also happened to be Nephy's mother. She had dropped by the other day, but because of the open hostilities with Bifrons, she decided to come back another time. Zagan was looking after the pendant, which was the only proof in the world that they were mother and daughter, and had yet to give it to Nephy. He wanted to give it to her in a nice atmosphere, like while on a date, so he ended up constantly putting it off. Orias was someone he deeply respected, and he couldn't really keep her or Nephy waiting much longer, so he had to hurry.

"No, no, no, it's not like I'm planning on causing you any trouble here, Mister Archdemon. If anything, it's, like, kind of awkward to show my face to my family, so I don't really wanna..." Selphy easily let her true intentions show, and Zagan shut her up with a single glare as he leaned back into his throne.

"...Well, whatever," Zagan muttered. All he wanted to do was try things couples would do with Nephy. And since he was already busy planning for that, he didn't feel like increasing his workload any. As he racked his brains over the matter for a while, Foll came tottering over and plopped down on his lap. It seemed she sensed that the serious talks were over, and came to get spoiled. And so, Zagan gently brushed the head of his beloved daughter.

Hm, if it's a gathering of all races on the continent, then it's not completely unrelated to Nephy and Foll... Foll's case was special. Dragons were said to have vanished from the world entirely, so it was possible that she was in fact the very last living member of her race. And in that case, it wasn't something she could just ignore to protect her current way of life. A dragon's lifespan far surpassed that of an Archdemon like Zagan, after all, so she would eventually have to live without him. And, as he brooded over that, Raphael nodded.

"It is about time for dinner. Give your damn life to your professional duties already," Raphael demanded as he stared at the siren.

"I, like, don't even do any of the cooking, remember?" Selphy replied.

"Hm... Now that I think of it, there's a legend in Liucaon where they cook mermaids into a dish called 'sashimi' that grants eternal youth."

"Why are you mentioning that now!?" Selphy screamed in terror as Raphael dragged her out of the throne room.

That damn Raphael, he's properly met up with Kuroka already... The tabaxi, Kuroka, was something like a daughter to Raphael. After the incident in town came to an end, Zagan instructed Raphael to go take care of things at the church, but he never heard whether or not they were actually reunited. Even if Raphael was his butler, Zagan didn't like to pry into the private life of others, and Raphael himself likely thought the topic awkward, so Zagan never brought it up himself.

In the end, I found out nothing about Azazel... Kuroka was a member of an organization called Azazel, but that wasn't the Thirteenth Sacred Sword itself. It seemed the Thirteenth had some sort of involvement with the elves, so he wanted to get some definitive information on it, but...

While he was thinking of such things and watching the two of them leave the throne room, Zagan noticed that Foll was looking up at him like she had something to say. And so, he gently brushed his beloved daughter's head and tilted his head to the side.

"So, what is it? You have something you wish to talk about, right?" Zagan asked. The other day, Foll had looked up at Zagan like this because she had a personal request. At that time, she was badgering him to read a picture book because he was being indecisive. Zagan questioned his daughter in as gentle a voice as he could, and Foll opened and closed her mouth several times as if she couldn't find the words to say. And, as he patiently waited for her to put her feelings into words, before long, Foll cut to the chase.

"Zagan, you know what?"

"Oh?"

And once more, silence. Still, it didn't take all that long this time for her to continue.

"Zagan, you told me that if I wanted power, I should steal it," Foll stated.

"Yeah, I did, didn't I?" Zagan replied. It was something he told her when she first came to the castle. At the time, he had yet to decide to make her his adopted daughter, and he had no intention of taking any disciples aside from Nephy. Thus he told her that. Now that Foll was officially his daughter, Zagan didn't have any problem teaching her sorcery, but...

I want Foll to experience an ordinary life filled with happiness... That was why Zagan didn't want to give her too great a power.

"...But you gave Gremory and Kimry power," Foll timidly continued.

"...I did," Zagan responded. He gave them the power to fight so that they could protect his subordinates from demons and the other Archdemons. Even though he told his daughter to steal power, he ended up granting power to his other subordinates. She was likely unhappy about that.

"I also... want power..."

"Don't make that face. I've also thought of a suitable power to grant you," Zagan said as he stroked Foll's head.

"...Really?"

"Heaven's Scale Snowfield," Zagan quietly muttered those words as he raised his hands into the air. With that, lights that looked like powdered snow filled the air. It was a variation of one of the two sorceries Zagan created to kill the other Archdemons. Heaven's Scale was defensive sorcery that created an invincible shield. The floating lights in the dimly lit throne room looked like twinkling stars in the dark night sky.

"So pretty..." Foll said with a sigh. Then, she looked up at the scenery in a trance for a while, but eventually cast her gaze down in discontent and asked, "Zagan, this is Heaven's Scale, the one used for defense, right?"

"It is. What about it?"

"I'd prefer... the one that burns... Heaven's Phosphor."

That was the other sorcery Zagan created, the fire that burned life itself, and turned anything it touched to ash, Heaven's Phosphor. It was a power that should have been sealed as a forbidden spell because it was so powerful. It was also the very same power that Zagan granted to Gremory and Kimaris. Having said that, those were versions that were adjusted for them, and couldn't compare to the one Zagan himself used…

Well, wanting power tends to come hand in hand with seeking out violence… It seemed that Foll wasn't pleased with the self-protection sorcery Zagan displayed. Still, he showed no signs of being offended, and stroked his daughter's head.

"Hear me, Foll. Do you know what is most important to a sorcerer?"

"…To become strong?"

"That answer gets you fifty points."

"I'm wrong?" Foll asked as she cocked her head to the side.

"What a sorcerer needs to prioritize above all else… is extending their lives. Most sorcerers, including myself, stained their hands with sorcery in order to continue living. Power can help you live, which is why we seek it. If we were to die, we would lose our knowledge and everything else with it. That's why we build up our strength to live."

That was why sorcerers possessed superhuman physical strength, tenacious skin which could stop a blade, brute strength that could tear apart steel, a heart that could endure running at full sprint for miles without running out of breath… Once one was able to reach such a stage, they were true sorcerers. And even with all that, you would only be a freshly hatched chick in the world of sorcery. To reach the extremities of sorcery that people like Gremory had attained, a person needed to dedicate another several hundred years to honing their craft. Zagan was the strange one for having reached the very peak of sorcerers while in his teens.

"Foll, you may end up living a longer life than me, but you're still young. For now, learn more ways to defend yourself. This shall become a new set of scales to protect your skin."

31

Foll wasn't so foolish that she couldn't understand the logic behind that. However, she also wasn't mature enough to just accept that on an emotional level.

"Can I not use Heaven's Phosphor... because I'm small?"

"That's right. Once you grow bigger, I'll definitely teach it to you," Zagan promised.

"...Got it," Foll replied. Her voice didn't make it sound like she was convinced in the least, but she likely felt that she could only nod as she was doing now. Foll jumped off of Zagan's lap, then tottered out of the throne room.

I ended up ruining her mood... Foll surely knew that Zagan hadn't said anything unreasonable. However, children couldn't always act logically. The privilege to complain so selfishly was something he granted to her alone, since she was still a child. That was why he gazed at her back in a loving manner as she walked away from him.

She doesn't hate me now, right?

He'd be completely lying if he said her behavior didn't hurt, but he just had to deal with it. And, after checking that nobody else was in the throne room, Zagan gripped his chest and squirmed about.

"So, you ended up running away from Master Zagan?"

After getting into a fight with their father, there was a limited number of places a child would run away to. And so, Foll ended up going to Nephy, just as one would expect. They were currently in the food cellar behind the kitchen. Since Selphy had come over to do her job, they ended up with enough hands to go around, and preparation for dinner was already complete. Even if they stayed and talked in the cellar for some time, it didn't seem like anybody would come and interrupt them.

"You don't need to make that kind of face. It's not like Master Zagan is belittling or bullying you, Foll." Nephy, who was squatting down in front of Foll to line up with her sight, gently brushed her head as she said that.

Is it that obvious? Foll thought as she touched her own face. The moment Foll came running into the kitchen, Nephy rushed over to her right away. She had intended to stay rather resolute, but it seemed like that hadn't worked. After pondering over the matter for a bit, she immediately found her answer.

I said I would sense what you want, right? Don't worry about every pointless thing... That was what Zagan had said when he made Foll his daughter. Both he and Nephy cherished Foll to the point where they could tell what she was thinking just by looking at her face. She understood that fact well.

"But Zagan taught you, Gremory, and Kimry... It's unfair that I'm the only one he won't teach," Foll said as she tightly gripped at the hems of her skirt. She knew she was in no way inferior to the rest of them, so the situation felt especially odd.

"Your hair has grown as a bit, hasn't it?" Nephy said as she started undoing Foll's braids.

"It has?" Foll replied. Thinking back on it, Foll had been residing in the castle for three months already. Her hair definitely must have grown longer, but she'd never even noticed... When Nephy drew a magic circle in the air with her finger, a comb manifested in her hand. It was rudimentary summoning sorcery.

"The reason Master Zagan is teaching me sorcery is because if he doesn't, I won't even be able to do simple things like this. Since he told you to steal it, doesn't that mean he acknowledges your abilities already?"

"That… may be the case, but…" Foll started replying to Nephy's words, but eventually trailed off.

"It's alright. Just as your hair has grown longer, you will also grow stronger, Foll. Someday, you will surely grow far stronger than me, or Miss Gremory, or Sir Kimaris… or maybe even Master Zagan…" Nephy said as she moved behind Foll and began combing her hair. Foll's untied hair went past her waist and right down to her thighs. The way her hair danced around her buttocks felt ticklish. When she came to this castle, her hair had only gone halfway down her back.

"Master Zagan says good things come to those who wait. There's no need to be impatient. We all love you so much already, Foll, so you can count on us for now," Nephy claimed as she stopped combing Foll's hair and suddenly hugged her from behind. Wrapped up by her tender warmth, Foll felt a sense of relief that took the strength out of her knees.

Is this what… a mommy is like? Foll's father was the great Wise Dragon Orobas. However, she knew absolutely nothing about her mother. Seeing as how she wasn't there when Foll was first aware of her surroundings, it was possible that she had long since passed away.

Nephy had an air about her that made Foll instinctively feel she was a mother. Zagan had a different way of dealing with her than Orobas, but she at least knew that he loved her… She knew that much… but Foll began trembling in Nephy's arms.

"I also... love Nephy and Zagan. I really love you two just as much as I loved father."

"Yes. I know," Nephy replied. However, Foll felt like she didn't really get it.

Because I love them so much... I want to protect them... She didn't like being only on the receiving end. Foll wanted them to depend on her. She wanted to be useful to them, and have them tell her 'You did well.' Those feelings had always been inside Foll, but she understood what Zagan and Nephy were saying. That was why she tried to remain patient. However, she was no longer able to endure it because of the incident several days ago. Zagan's castle was attacked by a chimera Bifrons sent. It had the fragments of the Demon Lord embedded in it, and was a repulsive and dreadful enemy. There was no way Foll stood a chance against it, but Kimaris had managed to slaughter it. Not only that, but there wasn't the slightest bit of damage to his surroundings, and he had done it on his own. Even though Foll could only tremble in place, he could defeat that monstrosity with ease. She had assumed they were equals, so his sudden growth was troubling. However, that wasn't the main issue.

When Zagan came back, in an unusual turn, he was quite injured. However, rather than worry about his own body, he praised Kimaris by slapping his bulky chest and saying 'You did well' with a smile on his face. Foll was jealous, and she also came to realize how truly powerless she was. It had been the same when Archdemon Orias attacked. She was completely useless. All of their enemies were defeated by Zagan's powerful fist.

I want to be of use to Zagan. And then... I want him to praise me... And yet, she was far too little right now. She wanted to return all his favors by protecting him, so why was she so weak?

Plus, I even ended up troubling Zagan again... She wasn't even being selfish, so why didn't it work out? If the only real issue was her age...

"...I want to hurry up and get bigger," Foll muttered those words to put her feelings in order, not because she was looking for help. However...

"Keeheehee, I heard everything!"

The problem child of a granny, Enchantress Gremory, kicked down the door and charged into the food cellar with vigor. She had twisted goat horns coming out of her head and was currently in the form of an old woman, wearing her usual pitch black robe. Though, in an unusual turn, blood was dripping down from her nose.

"Gremory... nosebleed..."

"Urgh... Too much love power has built up, huh? Allow me to say this. Lady Nephy... nice love power!" Gremory screamed those words and rubbed away at her face with her sleeve as she showed them a fully content expression. Then, she looked down at Foll and said, "Lady Foll. I have a way to grant that wish."

Foll could somehow imagine that this was an evil whisper that would bring along a terrible situation, but she was not in the right frame of mind to argue. So, in her stead, Nephy faced Gremory with a cold smile on her face.

"Miss Gremory, you wouldn't dream of doing anything that would cause Master Zagan trouble, right?"

Although her face had become relatively more expressive as of late, this girl still didn't emote much. So, when she said something with a smile like that, she had an intimidating air to her that even surpassed Zagan's.

"Eeek? I-I promise I won't, okay? I've been on my best behavior lately! There's no way I could do anything to trouble my liege!"

Seeing Gremory shrink back, looking on the verge of tears, Foll figured out the truth.

Zagan is the strongest, but Nephy is the scariest... In that moment, she decided never to do anything that might anger Nephy. However, her mind was also focusing on something else.

Can I... really get bigger?

Gremory's devilish whisper had a certain charm to it that made the thought remain at the forefront of Foll's mind.

Zagan had slipped out of his throne room in the middle of the night.

Alright, time to buy clothes for my date!

During dinner, Foll seemed unable to regain her composure and look Zagan in the eyes, but she showed no signs of taking offense to what had happened earlier in the evening either. Zagan wanted to believe that she would get over it after sleeping on it. He was worried, but his date with Nephy was only a week away, so he had no time to spare.

The sorcerers he passed all looked at him and said things along the lines of, 'Huh, Archdemon Zagan? Where are you going at this hour?' but the most Zagan ever had ever was nod at them. They may have been confused by his behavior, but it was fine as long as he wasn't discovered by someone noisy like Selphy or Gremory.

After he finished making sure that nobody was following him, Zagan cracked open his castle's gates and slipped through the opening. However, at that moment, something surprising happened.

"Oh no!"

He heard an adorable scream resound from behind him. And, as he turned around, he caught sight of the woman he loved most.

"N-Nephy?"

"Master Zagan…?" Nephy replied, her ears quivering in surprise as she looked up at Zagan. She was currently holding a lantern in her hand, and seemed to be on her way back from the garden.

All my plans will be ruined if Nephy finds out what I'm doing! He had to think quick, or he was doomed.

"Uhhh, what are you doing out at this hour?"

"Well, there was just a little something I was worried about, so…"

"Something you were worried about?"

"Um, it is not something that you need hear of yet, Master Zagan. I'm most likely just being a little paranoid… In any case, what are you doing at this hour?"

"Uh, I'm, um…" Zagan's gaze wandered about as he tried searching for an excuse, and he ended up looking up at the night sky. There was a thin moon hanging overhead, and the stars were twinkling beautifully.

Now that I think of it, the moon was just like this on the day we met… The moon was so thin that it felt like it would up and vanish, and Nephy stretched her hands out toward it, which made him follow suit. And that was why Zagan stretched his hands toward the moon once more.

"I ended up coming out here on a whim because of the night sky," Zagan proclaimed in a grand manner. His excuse was entirely vague, but strangely enough, it sounded a lot like him.

"It really is a beautiful night," Nephy said as she let her gaze follow Zagan's hands, then let out a deep sigh.

"Yeah. It reminds me of the night I first met you, Nephy," Zagan replied as Nephy nestled in close to his side and stretched out her hands to the moon as well. As always, her hands weren't grasping anything, but it sure felt like they were. Zagan was completely taken aback by the situation.

Huh? Isn't this like... a really good atmosphere!? It was a shame that he couldn't go buy clothes for their date, but this was more than enough to make up for that loss. Even at the best of times, the two of them were strangely conscious of each other, so moments like this where both of them were at ease were rather rare. Zagan looked down at Nephy's face.

"...Ah."

And at the exact same time, Nephy looked up at Zagan, meeting his eyes.

"A-Ahahahah!"

"Fufufu..."

Both of them let out dry laughs, then averted their gazes. This sort of exchange had repeated itself often lately... No, not just lately. It had been happening for nearly half a month.

This is bad! Pull it together, Zagan! Zagan mustered his courage and cast his gaze at Nephy's face again. Her embarrassment still seemed to be winning out, since she simply looked away and began twiddling her fingers despite noticing his eyes on her. Her cheeks were faintly flushed and her breath was white as she rubbed her hands together. Looking closely, Zagan noticed that she was wearing her usual maid outfit and didn't have a coat. And so, he spread open his mantle and pulled Nephy into it.

"Wha..." Nephy let out a shaky groan as Zagan wrapped her up in his mantle. And honestly, she wasn't the only one being ruled by her nerves.

H-Huh? Wait, isn't this the same as a tight embrace? He only meant to share his mantle with her, but he ended up holding her close as a result. Zagan never intended to act so bold, but it was too late to back out now.

Well, I mean, this much is just natural for a couple, right? Right!?

Surprisingly, Nephy didn't try to shake him off. On the contrary, she was lightly squeezing back on Zagan's robe.

"…It's warm."

"S-Sure is!"

Zagan didn't even know what he was agreeing with, but that was the best he could manage in the tense situation.

Would it be better if I find her a coat or something for our date? Zagan pondered as he felt Nephy's body warm up. The muffler he received from Nephy the other day was rather comfortable, and with that, it was possible to warm the two both of them at once. However, he didn't like the thought of getting it dirty, which was why he kept it safely tucked away.

After mulling over such thoughts for a while, Zagan looked over to the lantern Nephy was holding. And having noticed his gaze, Nephy held up the lantern with a curious look in her eyes.

"Is there something wrong with this?"

"No, it's just been a long time since I've seen one being used."

The last time he'd seen one was at Bifrons' evening ball. Back then, the swaying lights of the lanterns atop the ship created a suspect atmosphere. Sorcerers could see in the night without relying on any source of light. They normally used some light when reading, but even then, cheap candles were more than good enough. Before Nephy came to the castle, he would just create light using sorcery. Lanterns took a hand to use, so they were far too unwieldy for Zagan's tastes.

"My apologies. It seems I'm still inadequate..." Nephy ran her hand down one of her ears in shame as she said that. Nephy was a quick study, but she still only began learning sorcery a few months ago. Due to that, Zagan had forbidden her from using any long-lasting sorcery, which included any creation of light.

"There's no need to be ashamed. Candlelight has a certain charm to it, so isn't it fine?" Zagan claimed as he took the lantern from Nephy's hand. And as he held it up, the lantern illuminated Nephy's blushing face.

"...Yes. Thank you... very much..." Nephy responded as her ears quivered like she was unable to endure the swell of emotions within her. Then, Nephy leaned in against him, which drew Zagan's attention to the pendant in his pocket.

Isn't this the perfect moment to hand it over to her...? No, wait, if I give it to her now, the main purpose of our date will be lost... I know it's fine as long as she genuinely enjoys the date, but it feels like all my hard work will be for nothing...

After hesitating for a little while, Zagan decided to leave the pendant for later. Instead, he illuminated more of the garden with the lantern.

"Well, since we're both out here, why not take a little walk?"

"Yes, Master Zagan," Nephy stared back at him in surprise for a moment before saying that and returning a slight smile.

She won't get bored of just walking around, right? Baseless anxiety began building up within Zagan as he and Nephy walked through the garden hand in hand. The starry sky was beautiful, but it still wasn't enough to illuminate their steps. Zagan could see without a problem, but Nephy had to remain cautious lest she trip. And, as that thought crossed his mind, Zagan was reminded of what happened a little while ago and came to a sudden realization.

"Um, Nephy…"

"Yes? What is it?"

"Foll's upset, isn't she?"

It seemed he had hit the bulls-eye. Nephy's pointy ears straightened out with a snap, and her gaze began wandering around looking for an excuse. However, before long, she figured it would be useless to try to dodge the issue and opened her mouth to speak.

"I'm surprised… you could tell," Nephy softly muttered.

"Well, I just hurt Foll's feelings earlier, and the last time she fled the castle was on a night like this, wasn't it?"

It was something that happened back when Foll had first taken up residence at his castle. Because Angelic Knights were the ones who had killed her father and she had one right before her eyes, Foll fled the castle in order to obtain more power to fulfill her goals.

At the time, we got through things because it was all a misunderstanding, but Raphael still ended up severely wounded… That incident was the reason his butler had lost a hand.

"That child understands what you're thinking, Master Zagan. It's not like she fled or anything, but…" Nephy trailed off as she tilted her head to the side.

"But something happened," Zagan chimed in, finishing her sentence.

"…Yes. I'm not trying to place all the blame on her, but Miss Gremory seemed ready for some mischief."

That damn Gremory again? Zagan honestly felt that that granny was far too carefree.

"Well, Gremory can be a handful, but when it comes to distinguishing between doing right and wrong… she may not be the best judge… Still, she's not so foolish as to spoil my good mood. It should be fine to leave her be."

Besides, the image of a small child running off and clinging to a granny wasn't all that unnatural a scene.

"It would be good if things ended peacefully…" Nephy replied with an anxious look on her face, which made Zagan laugh in agreement.

"Actually, Foll was badgering me to teach her Heaven's Phosphor."

"Yes. She told me already."

"But, well, I gave Gremory a Heaven's Phosphor that only she can actually use, so she won't be of any help to Foll. I know that may anger her, but I promise I've at least tried to think of other things I can do for her. Besides, if I can't at least put up with my daughter's temper tantrum, then I have no right to call myself a father."

"I understand how you feel, Master Zagan. Accumulating power draws people closer to danger, so honestly, even I hate the idea of our daughter learning such things… However, I understand Foll's feelings as well," Nephy replied, then silently nodded before casting her gaze over to the lantern Zagan was holding and saying, "I want to become someone who can be of use to you, Master Zagan. And yet, I require the help of a tool for something as simple as walking down a dark path. As I am now, I don't even hold a candle to Miss Gremory or Foll."

"That's not true. I mean, you have mysticism and celestial mysticism, right?" Zagan rebutted. If it came down to a fair fight, especially in an environment with trees and rivers where she could borrow nature's power, Nephy could currently rival even an Archdemon. Though, if they actually fought, someone like Nephteros could probably have defeated her due to their gap in experience, but that was another matter entirely.

"That... isn't something I attained through my own efforts. I feel like I'm the only one who cheated when everyone else worked themselves to the bone to grow stronger, and I don't like it," Nephy said as she shook her head at his response. Mysticism was a power she was born with, and celestial mysticism was something she learned by seeing once. It took great talent to perform either of those feats, but it seemed that it was still difficult for Nephy to accept. That was why she could relate to Foll.

But if she could use her draconic powers better, she would grow far stronger... Unfortunately, Foll seemed fixated on improving her sorcery instead. It somewhat narrowed her vision, but it could also be said that gaining power a dragon did not normally possess was better for them in the long run. Zagan wasn't quite sure he agreed, but he couldn't refute the idea either.

"Do you understand now, Master Zagan? If you do, then please don't scold Foll," Nephy begged as she looked up to Zagan as if appealing to his kind heart.

"Like I'd ever scold her. I said I'd put up with her temper tantrum, didn't I?" Zagan responded with a laugh, but nevertheless, his words were filled with sincerity.

Did I react poorly earlier...? Foll's desire to become stronger was something he had known since they first met. And looking back on that, Zagan realized ignoring that facet of her completely and telling her to act the part of an innocent child was utterly selfish of him. Having said that, he still didn't think it proper to grant her access to a destructive power like Heaven's Phosphor.

"It's not like I haven't thought of what kind of power to grant Foll, though..." Zagan muttered with a groan. That was precisely why he created Snowfield, but unfortunately, that didn't seem to be what Foll wanted.

"Wait, what were you planning on granting Foll?" Nephy asked, sounding rather surprised. It seemed Nephy wasn't told about that part, as she stared back at Zagan with a blank expression on her face.

"Oh, about that… It's still incomplete, but…" Zagan raised his hand as he trailed off and activated Snowfield. In the blink of an eye, specks of light enveloped the area like stardust, and Nephy let out a sigh, completely entranced by the sight.

"How beautiful."

You're far more beautiful… Those words made it all the way up to his throat, yet he didn't dare voice them. Zagan came to a stop, and then demonstrated what happened when a mass of mana collided with Snowfield's lights.

"It's more than sturdy enough, but its far too complex to manipulate freely and it also forces the user to stand still."

"Is that really an issue when you're using it to defend against projectiles…?" Nephy asked. However, a moment later something dawned on her and she said, "I see… This is just practice for what you plan on teaching her next, right?"

"You really do have a good sense for sorcery, Nephy," Zagan replied. He was shocked that she managed to figure out his intentions even though he hadn't explained anything to her at all.

Nephy remained silent for a moment, gazing quietly at the snowy lights in the air before deciding to speak to him.

"It's all a bit of a haze, but I do remember it. You once used sorcery to create an enormous light, Master Zagan. This Snowfield has the same color," Nephy stated. Then, she suddenly thought of something and asked, "Master Zagan, are you controlling all of these Heaven's Scales individually?"

"No, there's nearly a thousand of them here. They're set up to move about on their own and are attracted to nearby outbursts of mana," Zagan replied. He was perfectly capable of controlling them all individually, but this had been designed with Foll in mind. There was no meaning in creating something she was unable to control. Though, in that case, it was possible to give it to her in an even more simple form…

"It seems the same circuit has been placed into each Heaven's Scale, so would it be possible to control them in clusters?" Nephy inquired as she continued observing each and every speck of light that formed Snowfield.

"In clusters?"

"Yes. Controlling them by splitting them into grouped clusters. Wouldn't using circuits to unify nearby Heaven's Scales around one leader work? That way, you could manipulate all of them just by controlling a few select clusters."

Zagan stared back at her in wonder. He was completely taken aback by her brilliant idea.

"I see. In that case, controlling it would certainly be simple, and it would make it easy to move around while using it… Good job, Nephy."

"I'm just glad to be of help."

"You always are… Still, I can't help but be surprised that you thought of that," Zagan said in a tone laden with admiration, which made Nephy cast her gaze to the ground shyly.

"I only thought of it because some celestial mysticism I used before worked like that. Plus, I could never hope to control a thousand Heaven's Scales at once, so my mind moved to figure out ways for me to use them."

Guess that means there are some things that are easier to figure out because you have trouble with them, huh? That fact left Zagan astonished. He was capable of individually controlling all one thousand Heaven's Scales, which was precisely why he was unable to think of a solution from the perspective of someone who couldn't. Nephy, on the other hand, lamented the fact that she was weak, but she was able to come to a conclusion that was foreign to him because of her weakness.

"It's those parts of you that best serve me, Nephy, so have more confidence in yourself." Zagan was delighted by her discovery, which made him press his face lightly against Nephy's cheek as he said those words.

"Wawawa?" Nephy exclaimed. And within Zagan's mantle, Nephy's ears quivered up and down violently. That made him think he had made some sort of mistake again, but he decided to put such thoughts aside for now.

After that, Nephy continued to make completely incomprehensible noises, but before long, she settled down and nodded resolutely. And then, she spread her arms out in front of Zagan and kicked off the ground. When she reached his neck, Nephy wrapped her arms around it and embraced him tightly.

"O-Oh?" Zagan muttered. This time, he was the one whose eyes were left darting about, since Nephy was clinging to him extremely tightly. It was extremely unusual for Nephy to take such a bold course of action, but it was more than welcome nonetheless.

What is this…? It's really soft and warm… I swear, this is the first time Nephy's expressed her love directly. I'm so happy that my heart might just jump out of my chest! Zagan happily returned the hug despite his nerves getting the better of him. The way Nephy's bright red ears twitched about as she hugged him reminded Zagan of when Nephy turned into a child, which made her utterly irresistible.

It may have been that turning into a child helped Nephy regain her original personality. And if that was the case, Orias' actions were more than justified. After all, there was no way the usually reserved Nephy would perform such a bold expression of her love without something changing within her.

"Um, Master Zagan," Nephy mumbled as she basked in the joyous moment.

"What is it?"

"I'm, um, extremely happy that we were able to go on a walk together like this late at night. Is that thing called a date… something similar?"

"Huh? Uh, I wonder…?"

This was a first even for Zagan, so he didn't know what exactly a date entailed. But at the same time, he felt that it had to have been something quite similar.

"Well, I'm sure it's like this, but even more amazing! We'll go to shops and streets we don't usually go to, dress up, walk around, and do something special!" Zagan proclaimed. By something special, he of course meant handing the pendant over to her.

At that, Nephy's pointy ears quivered with a twitch, and in an unusual turn, she formed a grand smile.

"Okay. I'm looking forward to it."

Zagan felt that he had just unnecessarily raised the bar, but he decided not to worry about it. Nephy seemed overjoyed, and in the end, that was all that mattered. Unfortunately for him, he had no way of knowing what calamity would befall him the very next morning…

"Zagan, I wanna get bigger."

The next day, Foll stopped by the throne room before breakfast. Behind her was Gremory, in the form of an old woman, with sweat pouring down her brow.

"Hm... Go on. Let's hear it," Zagan scratched his jaw and nodded as he gave her his reply.

"L-Lady Foll. I don't believe this is something we have to bring up to our liege all of a sudden. I mean, don't you think fools like Kimaris or Purgatory could lend us a hand instead as long as certain conditions are met?" Gremory whispered to Foll from behind in a flustered voice, clearly worried about Zagan finding out about her dastardly schemes.

"You said you can't do it, Gremory, so it'll be the same for everyone else. Zagan's the only one we can ask," Foll replied resolutely.

"No, well, you might have a point, but..." Gremory trailed off as she continually stole glances over at Zagan with a completely pale face.

The fact that Foll could speak frankly meant she trusted Gremory a fair amount. Zagan, personally, would have preferred it if they stayed farther apart, since Gremory could only ever be a bad influence on his daughter. Still, he had relied on Gremory and considered her his trusted retainer, so it would have been strange if he told Foll to avoid her.

In any case, she wants to get bigger... not stronger...? That could probably be done with the help of Gremory's sorcery, which manipulated one's age, but from the looks of things they hadn't succeeded yet. In that case, what exactly was the purpose of them telling Zagan everything? That wasn't a very hard question to answer, but Zagan decided to wait for his daughter to continue explaining herself as he stared at her. And before long, Foll gathered her resolve and opened her mouth to speak.

"Zagan, you think I'm too small to grant power, which means I just have to get bigger!"

"I see your point. And?"

Foll was a girl who liked to take action. If she had come to that conclusion, then she would make her idea come true and show off the results to Zagan. The fact that she hadn't already done so meant there was a reason she couldn't. And, as Zagan urged her to continue, Foll bit down on her lip in humiliation.

"But… it didn't work with just me and Gremory."

"I see. I've heard that dragons have tremendous resistance against sorcery. Sorcery meant for humans must not have been good enough," Zagan remarked. An ancient dragon's scales were said to be able to naturally repel sorcery, and even a masterwork sword couldn't leave a single dent on them.

Even putting that aside, dragons were incredibly powerful. Their speed and strength was unmatched, to the point where even Kimaris, who was known as the fastest being in the world, couldn't keep up with Foll while carrying people like she could. This especially applied to Foll, as she was a descendant of the legendary Wise Dragon Orobas. Frankly speaking, her latent potential easily dwarfed both Zagan and Nephy. And that was why, even though she was still a young dragon, it wasn't all that simple to manipulate her body. It wasn't the least bit surprising that it was beyond Gremory's capabilities.

"Help me, Zagan. I need to get bigger," Foll looked up at Zagan's face with a pleading look as she said that.

"…And once you're bigger, you want me to teach you Heaven's Phosphor?" Zagan asked.

Foll understood the reason Zagan wouldn't grant her power, failed in an attempt to overturn his decision, and still came to Zagan for help. That may have seemed silly to most, but Zagan didn't think her actions were at all unreasonable.

I guess this would be a good compromise… Foll found a means to gain Zagan's approval on her own. And after choking down her pride, she even went as far as to plead with Zagan for help. How could he possibly deny his daughter when she was working so hard?

Nephy's words from the night before rang through his mind, urging him on. *"However, I understand Foll's feelings as well."*

Zagan thought he understood Foll's feelings as well, so he had to respond appropriately. After being asked by both his bride and daughter, there was no way he could refuse. And so, Zagan returned a steady nod.

"…Very well, then," he declared.

"Really?" Foll asked as her amber eyes began sparkling.

"However, I have one condition. This is Gremory's sorcery, so the effect is temporary, right? I will decide when it is fine for you to become bigger. I forbid you to do it without my permission."

"Okay," Foll replied without a hint of hesitation in her voice. She had likely already predicted that such a condition would be attached. At this point, Zagan's expression finally loosened up.

"If you promise to keep to your word, then I'll teach you the 'Heaven's Phosphor' that burns all life."

Foll's eyes sparkled even brighter, and at that point, she leaped up and hugged Zagan's neck.

"Thanks! I love you, Daddy!"

"Ah!" Zagan let out a yelp in surprise. Foll's words made him so happy that he felt ready to keel over and cough up blood, but at the same time, he could tell that Foll had been brooding over the matter for quite a while, which made him hold it in.

I kind of wanted her to remain my little daughter for a while longer, though... Still, he knew that wasn't for the best. After all, what kind of parent would he be if he wasn't happy about his child's growth?

Thus, though they had yet to have breakfast, Zagan headed over to Gremory's lab.

"What do I need to do here, exactly?" Zagan asked as he walked into Gremory's lab.

A section of the castle had been allocated to Zagan's trusted retainers like Gremory and Kimaris. These rooms were generally used as labs where the sorcerers performed experiments and furthered their research. The castle was actually large enough to allocate rooms to all his subordinates, but most of them were using Zagan's other base, Archdemon Palace. He had suddenly gained around thirty subordinates at once, so managing all that was getting out of hand.

After arriving in Gremory's lab, he found a large magic circle that had already been prepared. Sorcery was something that differed in shape with infinite variations, but the fact that the magic circle was fully drawn out told Zagan that the sorcery itself had been perfected. However, that also meant that they didn't require Zagan's knowledge, which greatly confused him.

Taking in his astonishment, Gremory tapped the edge of her large scythe against the magic circle and began laughing creepily.

"The structure of the sorcery is complete. Plus, I've thoroughly investigated the optimal flow of mana through it, so there's no need to add any more circuits."

"I can tell."

Magic circles were woven together with crests called circuits, and Gremory's magic circle had over ten thousand of them crammed into it. Zagan didn't even know if he could put together such a delicately assembled magic circle himself, and that wasn't just because this sorcery was outside his area of expertise.

"Keeheehee, I see there's no need to explain my sorcery to you, my liege. What's lacking here is the mana necessary to surpass a dragon's resistance to sorcery. That is to say, we need power around the level of an Archdemon," Gremory said as she squinted her eyes in a pleased manner.

"That much, huh…?"

Honestly speaking, Zagan was taken aback. He thought he understood the power of dragons already, but it seemed they surpassed even his wildest imagination. She really was the legendary Wise Dragon Orobas' daughter.

In other words, they want me to use the Sigil of the Archdemon… It wasn't like Zagan's own mana surpassed theirs by a significant amount. The sigil on his hand was proof that he was an Archdemon, but in truth, Zagan didn't really find it desirable. That was why he only used it when needed.

It was borrowed power, a dangerous sigil that could turn its fangs against him at any moment. He had used it as a means to seal the sigil of another Archdemon, but he had no intention of relying on it for much more than that. However, it was also true that it was basically a container filled with a preposterous amount of mana.

Well, I guess it isn't a problem. I'll just be using it to amplify Foll's mana here...

"Let me get this straight. All you need is for me to send the mana from the sigil over to Foll, right?" Zagan asked.

"Exactly," Gremory replied.

"Fine. Then I'll just supply her with... huh? Hold on! You want me to supply her with mana!?" Zagan roared, clearly flustered. Some sorcery could steal mana from others, but from what he could see, Gremory's magic circle included nothing of the sort. Including such a needless feature in such a delicately put together magic circle was something only an Archdemon could do, so that made sense. However, that meant he had to supply mana to her in a primitive way that wouldn't interfere with the sorcery...

Are you telling me to kiss or have intercourse with my own daughter!? Sex was obviously out of the question, so that just left kissing. Still, there was no way he could do that.

I mean, I haven't even kissed Nephy yet!

"Zagan, what's wrong?" Foll tilted her head to the side like she couldn't really understand what was going on as she asked him that question.

"No, it's just that the means of supplying mana is..." Zagan faltered. There was no way he could explain such a thing to his young daughter. However, he had already promised to cooperate with Foll's desire to become bigger. And above all else, he wanted to help his daughter who was earnestly trying her best. Having said that, straight up kissing her without explaining anything was completely out of the question.

Incidentally, Gremory was raising a clamor going, "Wooo, nice love power! What'll you do, Archdemon!? It's time to show me your true potential...! Ah, I've got a nosebleed."

After worrying about it for a while, Zagan gave up on explaining.

"Listen, you're about to have someone else's mana poured into you. Are you really fine with that?" Zagan asked.

"I don't really get it… but it's fine if it's you," Foll replied. She was willing to force a growth spurt to gain power, so it was wrong of him to even ask such a thing.

Then, as a parent, there's no way I can back off now… Zagan was the youngest sorcerer in history to become an Archdemon, which came about as a result of his great mental fortitude. That was why he found his answer even while faltering. And then, placing a hand on Foll's shoulder, he addressed her quietly.

"Well then, Foll. You may close your eyes."

"O-Okay…"

She was obviously nervous. Her body stiffened as she shut her eyes tightly. And then, Zagan brought his face to hers.

"Uh, is he really going to do it? Wait, this kind of development is far too sudden. Love power is something that should accumulate over time. It needs to be more graceful and dignified! But even if I don't like it, seeing my liege about to commit a sin for love is enthralling… Aaaaaah, I want to stop him… No, I want to watch over him! Ugh, what do I do!?"

Gremory was probably trying to keep it to herself, but she was being way too loud.

Kimaris has low blood pressure and is no good in the mornings, huh…? In that moment, Zagan came to realize just how much that sorcerer had been helping him.

Even Foll looked to be making an irritated face, so Zagan obstructed all sound around them. He created a barrier to isolate those inside it from those outside. It had no defensive properties whatsoever, but even if lightning struck outside, they would be unable to hear it.

As the surroundings suddenly fell silent, Foll's body shook with a start. And in order to put his daughter at ease, Zagan put his lips to her forehead.

"Huh...?" Foll mumbled, opening her eyes in surprise.

In short, I just have to create a path for the mana! A kiss was required, so this was Zagan's answer to that difficult problem. Since he only needed to come in contact with her to send her mana, this much was enough.

"A kiss on the forehead... supplies mana?" Foll asked as she touched her forehead in confusion.

"Well, yeah."

"...I didn't know that."

Even though it was on the forehead, it seemed to be embarrassing for her. Foll's cheeks had turned slightly red.

Should I have properly explained it after all? Zagan wasn't confident he could regain her trust if that made her hate him. He was worrying himself sick over that dilemma when Foll spoke in such a quiet voice that it felt like it would vanish at any moment.

"Oh, that's not bad..."

"I-I see..."

Why had things gotten that awkward? Zagan continued to worry about the status of his relationship with his daughter when he realized the usually noisy granny was far too quiet.

Oh yeah, I put up a soundproof barrier... After taking down the barrier, Zagan and Foll were left speechless.

"THAT! WAS! WOOOOOONDERFUL! Phew... I see. For a little girl, a kiss on the forehead is truly the best approach. You're as masterful as ever, my liege. Ahhh, I'm going to die from an overdose of all this love power!"

Gremory looked to have turned white like a sheet and was about to drown in a pool of blood from her nosebleed.

"Zagan… Gremory's…"

"Don't look," Zagan said as he blocked his daughter's line of sight with his body.

"Keeheehee, I really thought that was going to kill me, but it looks like the preparations are complete," Gremory said as she got back up to her feet unsteadily.

"Is mana really being supplied here?" Foll asked while shaking her head as if she didn't believe it at all.

"Mm. Lady Foll, if you use sorcery now, you can pull mana from my liege's inexhaustible supply using that path he just created. Though it was simplified, it shouldn't be a problem."

"Your mana is being amplified. Give it a try," Zagan said as he nodded along to Gremory's words.

"…Okay!" Foll exclaimed as she nodded with vigor. Then, she stood in the center of the magic circle. After verifying that, Gremory began clearly chanting, and before anyone knew it, her figure had changed from that of an old woman to that of a beautiful young one. It was her in her prime, and the fact that it was necessary showed how powerful this sorcery was.

"[Time is the ring which circles from the moon to the sun. The spiral which stretches out toward the flow from high to low. That which governs over the beginning to the end. Thus, what binds the change from the sun to the moon, from low to high, and from the end to the beginning, shall also be time itself.]"

Her spell was similar to a Celestian chant, perhaps because she was once the pupil of Orias. And while Zagan was instinctively drawn in by that, he was assaulted by a sense of exhaustion from having his power suddenly pulled out of his body. Foll required more mana, and it was flowing out of Zagan's body at a rapid rate.

"Sigil of the Archdemon, lend me your power!" Zagan proclaimed as he held his right hand aloft. Suffocating mana swelled up in the area in an instant, and his sense of exhaustion dissipated.

Dragons have a rather terrifying capacity after all... Zagan believed the mana supply from the Sigil of the Archdemon was something that far surpassed the reach of man, but this situation made him realize there was a race that could easily consume it. Before long, a change began to show in Foll. Her arms and legs began stretching out, her hair spread out into the air, and her flat body began swelling. In other words, she was changing from a child into a woman.

Is it working? Zagan wondered. And at that exact moment...

"Ugh..." Zagan groaned as his vision distorted.

"Zagan!?" Foll yelled as she rushed over and supported him by the shoulder.

It's dangerous to interrupt such a delicate ritual... They were even pouring in mana from the Sigil of the Archdemon. If things went south, it could run rampant and destroy the entire castle... No, even Kianoides wouldn't be safe in the worst case scenario. That was why Gremory didn't stop chanting. She surely understood the situation and wished to avoid any danger. Her chant accelerated, hurrying the ritual on to its conclusion.

Foll looked anxious, but went back over to the middle of the magic circle. Her figure had already grown to about the same size as Nephy.

Hold on, isn't she getting a little too big here...? It was likely because he was crouching down, but Foll was now big enough that he had to look up at her. However, the one who looked even more bewildered than Zagan... was Foll.

"Zagan, you're…"

Before she could finish speaking, the magic circle shattered, leaving behind a dazzling light. It seemed the ritual was finished. There appeared to be a considerable burden on Gremory as well, as she was gasping for breath after her chant stopped.

Foll's body had grown large enough that her usual native dress couldn't remain intact. In human terms, she looked to be in the latter half of her teens. The same age or older than Zagan, basically.

"Ow…"

Children's clothing was far too small for her body now. The portions around her now striking breasts were especially unable to endure it, as a button shot off it and into Zagan's forehead. It seemed the ritual was a success for the time being.

"Zagan…" Foll tried to rush over to Zagan again, but…

"Ah!"

She wasn't yet used to her large body, and tripped on the way.

"Look ou— Huh?" Zagan leaped up to try and catch Foll, but for some reason his body didn't move as he wished. His daughter's body was far heavier than he imagined it was as it leaned down on him. He somehow made it in time, but the two of them ended up falling over together.

And since her breasts dropped down right over his face, he felt awfully hot… No, he didn't have the time to let his focus shift over to that. The suffocating pressure they were putting on him was a more pressing issue. Somehow, they were crushing him.

"MmmMmmMmm!"

"A-Are you alright, Zagan?" Foll asked in a shaky voice. She was trying to do something to improve the situation, but she couldn't move her body very well and was only capable of squirming about.

"Calm down. You're not used to the sensation yet. If you panic, it'll just get harder to move," Gremory said as she instructed Foll on how to control her new body. Having gotten her breathing back in order, she worked to free Zagan from the jaws of death. However, when she did, Gremory's face stiffened up completely in shock.

"Wh-What the hell is this!? Zagan… Wait, are you even Zagan?"

"What do you mean?" Zagan asked as he cocked his head to the side. And as he said that, he noticed that his voice was strange. It was usually far more low pitched than this, so the change surprised him.

And honestly, it wasn't just his voice. His clothes had become slack and felt just about ready to fall off. The reason he was unable to catch Foll was because he ended up stepping on the hems of his robe.

Thoroughly confused, Zagan looked down at his hands… only to find that his boorish hands were now small and pudgy.

Hey, what's going on here…? Zagan timidly touched his own face. It was all springy, and didn't feel much like his own face at all. And to make matters worse, Foll and Gremory looked completely dumbfounded, like they weren't sure they were even actually speaking to Zagan, and that really hurt him.

However, what stung most was that Zagan, who prided himself as a sorcerer with superhuman physical abilities, was unable to catch a girl in her teens. He could easily lift up Foll when she took on her dragon form, so how was that even possible?

Looking around his surroundings in exasperation, Zagan spotted a jug of water in the corner of the lab.

What the hell happened here… And, as he peered into the jug in an attempt to get some answers, all the color drained from his face.

Unfortunately for him, the reflection in the water showed a young child who looked an awful lot like Zagan.

"It has been a long time, young man."

So he said as he looked down at the tiny old man standing beneath his eyes. No, the old man wasn't really all that small. It was just that he was far too large. He was large enough to easily step over this old man, which clearly made him larger than any human being. This was a thought that passed his mind while his consciousness was in a haze. This was a dream. And in this dream, he had become someone else.

A faint smile could be spotted through the gap in the old man's hood.

"I'm sure all humans look like children from your perspective, but it's odd being called a young man at my age. You also dislike being called a giant lizard, right?"

And he raised a hearty laughter in response to the old man's cynicism.

"Hahaha, you are the only one who dares to speak to me in such a frivolous manner... Come now, there's no need to take offense over such a trivial jest."

The old man let out a small sigh in response to his delighted attitude.

"And you're about the only one who can still make me sigh... In any case, it's been about a thousand years since then, huh?"

The old man's words pricked at his heart. He felt lonely, and the only one who could possibly understand that feeling was this old man. However, he simply narrowed his eyes.

"Speaking of a thousand years, I found a girl who closely resembles 'her' the other day," the old man said as if remembering something.

"Hm… Could she be… a high elf?"

"Yeah. Seems to be a case of atavism. Still, this girl has splendid white hair nonetheless. Over the past thousand years, 'she' was the only one who could compare to such a level of purity. Our young ones seem to want to know more about her, so I ended up sheltering her."

Listening to the old man, he closed his eyes, reveling in nostalgia. What came to mind was the image of a human boy, a man, and a lone girl. It was an extremely old memory, so their faces and clothing were all a blur. It wasn't clear exactly what they were to him, but they stayed in his heart to the point where simply thinking of them made him happy. That was why he didn't laugh at the old man's actions, but instead nodded pleasantly.

"I would like to meet her at least once. I did not get a chance to exchange words with that one a thousand years ago."

"It'd be nice if you could. It seems that she needs saving. However, I'm unfortunately not very well suited to such a thing."

"Such troublesome matters."

"Is it not you dragons who guide mankind?"

He let out a groan upon hearing the old man's reply. And then, after a short pause, he quietly raised his face.

"If I possessed such power, then this would never have happened."

He and the old man looked off into the distance where the world began distorting. That which should not exist was trying to manifest in the world. And seeing that sight, the old man formed a faint smile once more.

"You can surely guide them. That's why Solomon, 'she,' and I were all happy. That's precisely why we despaired, and thus struggled against them," the old man said, his voice laden with gratitude. Then, he asked, "Now that I think of it, you had a daughter yourself, right? Is she in good health?"

"She is but a chick who has just learned how to walk. However, she will one day be the last dragon in this world. It makes me think I may have done something cruel."

"The last dragon…" the old man muttered before continuing in an affectionate tone, "I would also like to meet that child."

"Then so shall it be. Meeting you would be a good opportunity for her to learn of the world," the dragon said as he silently looked up and stared at the distortion before them. Then, he spoke glumly, stating "Azazel is broken, and we have not even half the Sacred Swords here. The only Sigil of the Archdemon we possess is the one on your hand. It shall not go like a thousand years ago." And despite all that, he smiled as he said, "But, 'tis a good day to die."

The old man opened his mouth in surprise, then returned a laugh.

"Until we meet again, Wise Dragon Orobas."

"I look forward to meeting that high elf who closely resembles her, Archdemon Marchosias."

This was a scene from a little before Zagan and Nephy first met. It was a lost memory that none in the world knew of.

"What is the meaning of this, I wonder?" Nephy asked. Her voice was usually a quiet one, and yet now it had a sharp ring to it like thunder. At a glance, there didn't seem to be even a hint of anger on Nephy's face. Compared to her usual expressionless self, one could even say she was smiling. And yet, Foll and Gremory, who were made to kneel before her, were both cowering.

"...Sorry."

"Y-You've got it all wrong, Lady Nephy. I had nothing but the best inten... Yes, I'm very sorry..."

They were currently in the throne room. Nephy went out to look for Zagan and the others when they didn't show up for breakfast, and after discovering Zagan in his child-like state, she began interrogating the two culprits, Gremory and Foll. She was currently seated atop Zagan's throne in his stead, looking down on the two of them with a cold smile... However, the ground at her feet had suddenly become covered in moss. It seemed Nephy's mysticism activated when she got all worked up. There was no need to even ask now, since it was clear she was in a bad mood.

I haven't seen Nephy this angry in a long time... Right after Zagan and Nephy had just met, they were attacked by Angelic Knights and Zagan was wounded in the battle. That was the first time Nephy used mysticism in front of him. This wasn't quite as severe as that time, but her anger was still palpable.

Honestly, I really didn't want her to see me like this... Zagan's worst nightmare had come true. There were things about his past that he didn't want her to know because he loved her. He hadn't exactly lived an honest life back then, so having such a vivid reminder of his past shoved in her face pained him.

Foll was no longer able to wear her usual native dress, so she was borrowing clothes from Gremory. Unfortunately, they were a bit too provocative, since they were the clothes Gremory wore when she returned to her prime. Looking at her, it was clear that Foll was an eighteen-year-old woman. Zagan, on the other hand, didn't even look ten. It seemed their ages had been swapped. Or at least, their physical ages, anyway, since it was hard to compare a dragon's lifespan to a human's.

Incidentally, Gremory fully understood that she couldn't try to trick Nephy by taking on the form of an old woman or a little girl and was seriously facing her in her prime form, but her face was drenched in sweat. Between Foll and Gremory, it seemed that Gremory would be the first to completely break down if this kept up, so Zagan cleared out his throat with a cough.

"Um, Nephy…? It's not like Gremory was just fooling around, okay? This is also my fault, since I didn't control the Sigil of the Archdemon properly, so don't be too mad…" Zagan implored her for mercy on their behalf. Though, even he hesitated to cut into the conversation initially. And, as he tried to mediate in a weak-willed fashion, Nephy tightly embraced him.

"But for Master Zagan to become so adora… so small like this…"

"What were you about to say just now? Actually, can you let me down already?" Zagan asked. Even he was reduced to complaining in such a situation. That was because Nephy was hugging him like a stuffed doll and wouldn't let go. Zagan had initially thought of hiding. However, when he was caught in this unsightly form by the person he most wanted to hide it from, he froze up on the spot. Eventually, he came to… and it ended up like this.

By the way, there were no children's clothes whatsoever in the castle, so Zagan was still wearing his now baggy robes. Thanks to that, he was unable to move properly, and couldn't even escape from Nephy's lap. Looking upon that scene, Gremory grasped her chest and gave him a big thumbs up.

"Hnnngh, nice love pow— Erk, n-no, it's nothing."

Why was this granny unable to learn her lesson? Gremory was reduced to a trembling mess as Nephy glared at her with a cold gaze that felt like a dagger of ice. The scariest part of all was that Nephy was still smiling the whole time, which made even Zagan break out into a cold sweat.

In any case, she knew the situation wouldn't get resolved even if they continued bullying Gremory, so Nephy pinched at her brow as she cut to the chase.

"...Well, from what I've gathered, you're unable to return Master Zagan to normal, correct?" Nephy inquired. The three of them had performed a ritual to help Foll grow older. The fact that Zagan also became younger was an unforeseen side effect. When mana that was separated from the control of circuits ran wild, it often transformed into a 'curse' that differed in nature from sorcery. In such a case, even Zagan's ability to devour sorcery could not nullify it. Normally, anyone who possessed as much mana as an Archdemon wouldn't get cursed, but...

"My liege's and Lady Foll's power both went berserk at the same time. That is already something outside the realm of sorcery. I can't return him to normal with my power... If I say this is a situation where a dragon and an Archdemon collaborated to cast a curse, would you understand?" Gremory said with a humiliated expression on her face.

"A curse..." Nephy mumbled. Back in the hidden elven village, Nephy was ostracized as a cursed child, so that word made her body tremble.

Even Gremory looks depressed... Normally, she just screwed around without a care in the world, but there was still no mistaking the fact that she was a powerful sorcerer. Not only had her specialized sorcery run wild, but she was unable to put things back in order. It truly must have been humiliating for—

"Even though I brought about such an awesome display of love power, I can't even reproduce it! How humiliating!"

"Miss Gremory," Nephy said flatly.

"...Sorry. I'm joking. I shall devote my body and soul to finding a way to fix this," Gremory replied. Nephy's emotionless voice had reduced Gremory to prostrating herself on the ground, begging for forgiveness. Nephy, on the other hand, looked to be having a headache, and was pinching her brow once more.

"For the time being, explain this in a way that even an amateur like me would understand," Nephy asked. It was only natural that Gremory was unable to do anything but make incoherent noises with Nephy on her case, so Foll spoke on her behalf.

"Zagan wouldn't give me power because I'm small, which made me decide to get bigger. But we didn't have enough power with just me and Gremory, so I asked Zagan to help out."

Nephy looked troubled, seemingly not sure how to react to the fact that her daughter was now bigger than her.

"And then we failed, and this happened," Foll said as she held up the back of her right hand. The Sigil of the Archdemon that Zagan possessed floated up on the back of Foll's right hand. However, he looked down at his own hand, and spotted the sigil woven of mana was still there. The one on Foll's hand was the same in that it was woven with mana, but it was more like a birthmark than anything.

"This is likely something known as a stigma. Since I opened a path to share mana with Foll, the sigil was transcribed on her hand," Zagan stated.

"A stigma…?" Nephy said, tilting her head to the side.

"It's a phenomenon where your scar shows up on somebody else as if it's theirs. Seems they treat them as something sacred in the church, but it's troublesome when these show up on sorcerers. If handled poorly, it's entirely possible that once one of you dies, the other will have to tag along for the trip… Having said that, the path I opened with Foll is a one-way street. If there are any effects, it'll likely only transfer from me to you."

"Could it be… Is that what this nice, warm feeling on my back is?" Foll asked as she looked about in confusion.

"Ah, it probably is," Zagan replied. Since Zagan was sitting on Nephy's lap and couldn't get away, an indescribably pleasant sensation ran up his back. The reason he was unable to calm down was because he noticed the things pressing into him.

"Anyway, my mana is currently flowing to Foll without any restrictions. That's probably the cause of this ridiculous age swap. Makes sense, since all of this went wrong during Gremory's ritual."

The core problem was the stigma of the sigil that Foll showed them. Foll's body had grown, but it wasn't like there was any effect on her mind, so her explanation was a little lacking. And after Zagan supplemented her explanation, Nephy nodded in a convinced manner.

"We used the Sigil of the Archdemon to amplify sorcery that originally had no effect on a dragon. It was my carelessness that allowed it to run rampant like that. It's meaningless to blame Gremory at this point."

"...My liege. Aren't you strangely fixated on that point? It isn't like I'm the only one being blamed here," Gremory asked. However, Zagan completely ignored her peculiarly discontent voice, and continued his explanation.

"I came to the throne room because I thought that if I recovered some of my powers, I'd be able to find a solution, but... well, it looks like that won't work."

There were countless barriers that strengthened Zagan's powers surrounding his domain. And the place where his power was strengthened the most was his throne room, but it seemed the situation was far more troublesome than he initially thought, since returning here didn't change anything.

Nephy was listening to his explanation intently, but she was unaware that she was stroking Zagan's head the entire time. Moreover, he found it unexpectedly comforting and didn't bluntly tell her to stop either.

I feel like I understand Foll a little more now... Being treated like a child should have proved vexing, but there was something so comfortable about it that he just couldn't resist.

"Wait, does that mean your powers have weakened, Master Zagan?" Nephy remarked, completely taken aback.

"Shhh..." Zagan whispered as he put his index finger up to his lips, then said, "Well, I'm not quite as powerful as before, yeah. For example, if I had to rebuild the barrier around this castle, it would take several days instead of several minutes. And right now, I may not even be able to devour sorcery depending on my opponent's abilities."

As he was, even the Heaven's Phosphor he intended to teach to Foll was out of reach. They couldn't allow such a fact to be known by others, so Nephy covered her mouth in a panic. Fortunately, the

71

only ones present here were Zagan, Nephy, their daughter Foll, and Gremory. Gremory was a trusted retainer of Zagan's, so he could assert that she wouldn't speak of this to others. Having said that, it didn't change the fact that Zagan was in a rather perilous position.

"Master Zagan…" Nephy muttered in a grief-stricken voice, then cocked her head to the side as if a certain doubt just came to mind before saying, "If the source of this incident is the one-way street, why not change it to go both ways?"

Well, even if they didn't kiss on the lips, they could get the same result if Foll kissed Zagan's brow or cheek or something to open the other path. However, Gremory simply shook her head.

"Did I not say already? This is a curse, not just some simple malfunction. Actually, the fact that the flow of mana is only one-way may be precisely what's keeping it from getting any worse. There's a chance we'll throw off the balance of the situation if we act too rashly."

"What could happen if we do?"

"In the worst case, Zagan may die."

Nephy gulped down, then squeezed Zagan tighter.

Well, can't say I blame her. I would make the exact same face if someone told me that Nephy was in grave danger…

"In other words, it's completely different from when I became smaller… right?" Nephy wrung out those words in a trembling voice.

"Though I regret to say it, you are correct."

Back when Nephy was transformed into a child, every aspect of the sorcery was under the complete control of Archdemon Orias. In that sense, it was safe.

And as he mulled over such things, a thought came to mind.

Hm? Orias is Gremory's teacher, right? In other words, Orias and Gremory used the same sorcery, and as an Archdemon, Orias' power and experience was on an entirely different level. She was the one who turned Nephy into a child before, and her power encompassed both sorcery and mysticism. It may have been possible for her to do something about this troublesome curse. Gremory also seemed to have realized that possibility, and stared fixedly into Zagan's eyes.

"Let's see… Shall we rely on your teacher?"

"I'll try to get in touch with her."

"Master Zagan, are you acquainted with Miss Gremory's teacher?" Nephy asked, looking astonished by their exchange.

"Huh? Ah…" Zagan was at a loss for words upon realizing that his statement was rather careless.

Crap. If I tell her I'm going to rely on Orias, Nephy will definitely tag along. Even now, she was hugging him so tightly that it was clear she never wanted to let him go. There was no way she would allow him to travel alone in his current state.

Orias was Nephy's actual mother. However, Nephy's memories of that fact were hazy, and she still didn't know the truth. Zagan had met her by chance the other day, but because of the ongoing dispute with Archdemon Bifrons, they ended up parting ways there for the time being.

That was why Zagan didn't want their reunion to be under such grim circumstances. And while he was racking his brain for a solution to the problem at hand, Gremory shook her head in a grave manner.

"My teacher is also an Archdemon, so my liege has met her in the past. However, it may be better for you not to meet her, Lady Nephy."

"Why is that?"

"Did I not say so already? She is my teacher. The very same teacher who drilled the essentials of love power into me. A high elf like you, who is full of love power, may not get away from her safely."

"Eeek…" Nephy screamed, seemingly left at a loss for words.

Hey! Stop that! It'll just make things even more complicated when Nephy and Orias meet again! However, they now had a reason to keep Nephy at a distance. And though it pained him greatly to do so, Zagan gave a slight nod to affirm Gremory's statement.

"…You're quite correct. Even I can imagine what would happen if that Archdemon were to meet Nephy," Zagan said, meaning he could imagine the heartwarming reunion between mother and daughter.

"Is it alright for that kind of person to meet Master Zagan when he's in this adorable form?" Nephy added timidly.

"Huh? Uh, I wonder…? My teacher has no interest in mankind, so I think it should be fine."

Hey! Don't actually sound worried! And Nephy, don't call me adorable! Zagan believed that Orias was a perfectly respectable person. He had no confidence that he could pay respect to that old woman if she started blurting out things that Gremory often said like love power. And though she had turned pale from all the talk, Nephy still mustered her willpower.

"Let's talk through all our options. What are your thoughts on how to return Master Zagan to normal?"

"Like I said, relying on my teacher is our first option. My age manipulation sorcery is something my teacher developed, so she would be best suited to help," Gremory said as she stuck up a finger to start counting the options. When she lifted her second one, she said, "Next is to somehow sever the path that was created earlier.

However, this runs a similar risk to reconnecting the path, since it's possible to cause a further outburst of mana that could endanger both their lives. We may think of it as an option, but it should be our last resort."

Nephy held her breath as she nodded, and Gremory raised a her third finger in response.

"And finally, we can rely on techniques from another continent."

"Another continent…?"

Gremory simply nodded as Nephy tilted her head to the side.

"All sorcery on this continent shares the same root. Nothing more can be done with it if my teacher is unable to return him to normal. However, power that differs from sorcery exists on the island nation of Liucaon. That's why there's some value in shifting our focus over to it."

"In that case, can't something be done with Nephteros' mysticism or even celestial mysticism?" Nephy replied.

"Perhaps, but I think that may be hard. Mysticism is certainly powerful, but you and Nephteros don't have full control of it. As for celestial mysticism…" Gremory hesitated to speak any further. However, Zagan, and even Foll, understood what it was she was trying to say. That was why his now-grown daughter hesitated as she opened her mouth to speak.

"I feel like… celestial mysticism is a power that only exists for battle…"

In a fight, it was an overwhelming force that could obliterate a castle in a single blow. Combine that with its healing power, and celestial mysticism was far too powerful. It was as if it was a weapon developed to fight something beyond human understanding.

Upon hearing that, the tips of Nephy's ears quivered greatly.

"A power... that only exists for battle...?" Nephy repeated in a hesitant voice. Sorcery was originally a means for sorcerers to fulfill their desires. It wasn't a power developed for the purpose of destruction or battle. However, because there was a direct connection between gaining knowledge and gaining power, all experienced sorcerers ended up becoming powerful. In a way, Zagan was a freak among the freaks, since he had only ever developed his sorcery to become more powerful.

Although Nephy was still a beginner, she understood that fact. And because of that, her eyes widened in shock.

Oh, I see. She must be thinking her power is only meant to hurt others... Zagan cleared out his throat with a cough in an attempt to grab her attention. And then, once he succeeded, he began to speak.

"Don't misunderstand, Nephy. Most technology in the world is unlike sorcery in that it was developed during times of war. Conflict gave rise to skilled swordsmiths, and their efforts gave birth to techniques like forging and casting. Then, those techniques, in turn, gave rise to the development of farming tools, metal fittings, and all sorts of other things."

"Is... that true?"

"It is. Essentially, Foll's saying that celestial mysticism is currently in that preliminary stage. She just means it's something that has yet to be applied in other fields. Isn't that right?" Zagan asked as he looked over to Foll, who nodded her head with a bob.

"Yeah. That's why even though celestial mysticism is strong, it isn't suited for delicate matters," Foll replied.

Nephy's expression loosened up as she heard that. And then, for some reason, she began petting Zagan's head.

"Fufufu, thank you for cheering me up, Master Zagan. You're certainly smart."

"N-Nephy? Why are you treating me like a child?" Zagan began whining.

"My apologies. It almost felt like I was dealing with Foll," Nephy responded with an apology, though that still didn't make her stop petting Zagan's head.

This doesn't feel bad, but... This wasn't the first time Nephy had brushed his head, but before she did so in a far more reserved manner. Right now, she was acting rather bold, to the point where it felt like his entire body was being caressed. As a result, Zagan unintentionally let out a satisfied sigh.

"Huh!? No, now's not the time for this!" Zagan yelled as he regained his bearings.

Forget the date, I won't even be able to buy clothes for it like this! He only had a week left to prepare, so time was of the essence.

"We have no time to spare, Gremory! Get in contact with Orias immediately!"

"As you wish," Gremory replied. Then, she stood up and gave him a deep bow before walking out of the throne room.

Zagan looked up at Nephy after seeing off his trusted retainer.

"That's the situation, Nephy. I've got a little business to attend to, so I'll be leaving the castle. Take care of the place while I'm gone," Zagan ordered as he sat atop her lap.

I need to make full preparations for when Nephy and Orias finally reunite!

"As you wish…" Nephy sounded somewhat taken aback as she responded. And she simply nodded as he jumped off her lap.

"What's wrong?"

"Master Zagan, meeting another Archdemon in such clothing is a little…"

Zagan's usual robes were far too large for him in his current form. Frankly, it looked less like clothing and more like a large blanket.

"Why not wear my clothes, then?" Foll inquired as she clapped her hands together.

"…Do you know what you're saying, Foll?" Zagan replied, sounding completely exasperated. It was true that her clothes would fit his new size, but there was no way he could wear girl's clothing. Even Nephy shook her head at the idea.

"I would enjoy seeing that, but he needs formal clothing."

"Hold it, Nephy. What do you mean you'd enjoy it?" Zagan asked. She'd been acting rather strange since he reverted to his young form, which had him confused. However, no one present paid her behavior any mind.

"It's my fault that Zagan shrunk, so I'll head into town to look for clothes," Foll gallantly volunteered to take action, but that just made Nephy's ears quiver anxiously.

"Will you be alright on your own?"

"I'll do my best."

Even if her body was now bigger, Foll was still Zagan and Nephy's young daughter on the inside, which was why both of them were nervous about the thought of her traveling alone.

"I'll tag along. Maybe we can even meet Orias while we're out there and save some time," Zagan replied. There was no guarantee Orias would be able to treat him on the spot, but it was still worth a shot. Zagan had to try to resolve his size issue as soon as possible, since he had a date coming up that was now in jeopardy.

"Before that, Nephy," Foll said.

"What's the matter?" Nephy asked.

"My feet are all numb…" Foll replied, her amber eyes on the verge of tears after being forced to sit on her heels this entire time.

Well, her senses haven't quite caught up with the new length of her limbs yet… She even needed Gremory's help to get changed at the moment. Left with no other choice, Nephy rushed over to Foll.

"You may be bigger than me now, but you're still a needy child," Nephy said in an affectionate tone. She was the very picture of motherly love.

Nephy grabbed Foll's extended arms and somehow managed to pull her up. And after she did, it was readily apparent that Foll was the taller of the two. She wasn't a whole head taller, but Nephy still had to look up to meet her eyes.

"I'm the bigger one now, so does that make me the mommy?" Foll curiously cocked her head to the side as she asked that question.

"I don't think our ages are all that different, though…"

"Hm, then how about I be the big sister?" Foll's eyes were sparkling with excitement as she said that, which left Zagan confused.

I guess nothing aside from her size has really changed… Foll was also quite pleased when the little Nephy called her 'big shis' back at the hidden elven village. Normally, she was always the smallest one around, so she must have enjoyed the feeling.

Immediately following that, the sound of something ripping resounded through the air.

"Oh, my clothes tore again," Foll muttered dryly. The moment she puffed out her chest, her clothes found themselves unable to contain her body and tore at the seams.

"What should I do? I got these from Gremory…" Foll drooped her shoulders dejectedly as she said that. And Zagan, in turn, simply tapped his tiny heel against the ground. Then, a magic circle spread out at Foll's feet that made the torn fibers around her chest reassemble. It was elementary sorcery, but Foll went 'oooh' in a surprised voice.

"How did you do that?"

"…Huh? Is this the first time you've seen it? It's basic sorcery, so I'll teach you later."

"Wow… Good boy!" Foll exclaimed as she started gently patting Zagan's head.

Goddammit… I can't believe my own daughter's treating me like a child… Zagan puffed out his cheeks to pout right as Foll looked down at her own chest in a troubled manner.

"I don't get it. Why did it tear? I've never had this problem before…" Foll mumbled in confusion. It seemed like she still didn't know all the ways her body had grown.

It's a little embarrassing for me to explain… Zagan thought as he went over what to say in his mind.

"Um, it's a little hard to explain, but you've grown up. And maybe because you're a dragon, you've swelled in certain areas more than Gremory has…"

That's far too direct. What the hell am I saying!? Zagan was left at his wit's end by the problem, but Foll simply opened her eyes in surprise.

"Your clothes can't endure it when your powers swell? I didn't know that."

"Oh… Well, it's something like that," Zagan said as he gave up on explaining it. Then, Nephy put her hand to her mouth while her ears quivered about in delight.

"In that case, both of you need to go get some new clothes. Foll, please take care of Master Zagan," Nephy requested. And with that, Foll looked at Zagan, her eyes filled with expectation.

"Zagan, I'll do my best as a big sister!"

"Mm. I'm expecting much of you."

A smile bloomed on Nephy's face as she watched the two of them. And at that exact moment, a quiet knock rang out from the door to the throne room.

"Who is it?" Zagan asked.

"It is I, my liege," Raphael replied.

"You didn't show up for breakfast, so I came to call you... Is there some sort of problem?" Raphael questioned Zagan in a silent voice from the other side of the door.

Well, it's probably fine to tell Raphael... They were on good enough terms for Raphael to give him tips for his date, so he knew he could rely on him.

"Are you alone?"

"Indeed."

"Then come in."

Raphael opened the door without making a sound, then stepped into the throne room as if slipping through the crack. He looked around, and after noticing Zagan and Foll's current states, his eyes shot wide-open.

"You are... my liege? And Foll?"

"That's right," Zagan answered his question, then went on to give him a summary of what happened.

"Oh my... What a troublesome affair."

"It's not that we have no leads. I hate the idea of putting myself in debt to another Archdemon, but I'm sure Orias can help."

"Is that so…" Raphael muttered as his expression gave away the fact that there was a problem on his mind beyond the situation itself.

"Did something happen on your end?"

"…No, it isn't anything that serious. More importantly…" Raphael trailed off as he looked to Zagan, then Foll, then Nephy and continued with, "What will you do about breakfast?"

"…Oh!" they all exclaimed in unison. They'd forgotten that Nephy had originally come to call them for breakfast. A sorcerer could easily go a whole day without eating food, but the option of not eating the breakfast that Nephy and Raphael had prepared wasn't even something any of them considered.

"Sir Raphael. Can you bring it over to the throne room for us?" Nephy asked in a resolute tone.

"Understood. I shall also order those damn servants not to approach the throne room."

"Good idea," Nephy replied. Zagan and the others were in awe at his ability to read a step ahead. Shortly thereafter, he returned with their breakfast in tow.

"I shall return later to take the dishes, so you may just leave them there," Raphael stated before he left the throne room once more. The room was equipped with a small table used for tea time, which suited their current needs just fine. After taking her seat, Nephy scooped up Zagan and placed him on her lap.

"H-Hey, what's the big idea?"

"It will be hard for you to eat with such baggy clothing. Allow me to assist you," Nephy responded as she picked up a spoon with Zagan still on her lap.

"I can handle eating on my own!"

"You're heading out after breakfast, so please at least rely on me at times like this."

Zagan found himself unable to act strong when faced with Nephy's desperate pleas. He desperately wished to resist, but he gave in to her whims instead.

"…Just this once, okay?"

"Yes!"

"I want that," Zagan said as he pointed at a bowl of soup.

"Okay, here you go," Nephy replied as she joyfully scooped up some soup with the spoon in her hand and carried it over to Zagan's mouth.

Gaaah! I'm happy, but also embarrassed! He found his childish figure utterly miserable. Who knew that being treated like a child would cut so deep? However, since Nephy looked extremely happy about the turn of events, he couldn't show his displeasure.

Foll's breathing grew more rough and nasally as she heard their exchange.

"Zagan, have some bread."

"Hey, why are you doing this too…?"

"You should listen to your *big sister*," Foll obstinately emphasized the words 'big sister,' which left Zagan with little choice. He opened his mouth despite cringing on the inside, and his daughter took that chance to toss some soft bread into it.

"Is it tasty?"

"It's food that Nephy and Raphael made. Do you even need to ask?"

"Wow… Good boy!" Foll exclaimed as a satisfied smile erupted onto her face.

Should I just act as their toy during meals...? It pained him to be treated like a child, but both his bride and daughter looked happy. Plus, it wasn't like the two of them were making fun of Zagan. He could tell that they truly derived great joy from the situation, which left him with little to complain about. That was why he pointed at the next dish he wanted with minimal resistance.

"I want dessert next."

"But there's still some salad left, Master Zagan," Nephy replied. He couldn't tell whether she wanted to spoil him or be strict with him as Nephy broke out into a smile and scooped up some pudding into her spoon.

"Zagan, you can have my pudding too."

He didn't intend to be greedy, but Foll also stuck out her spoon like she couldn't wait any longer.

Well, I guess this isn't all that bad... A king had to keep acting like one despite any adverse circumstances.

However, from the outside, the scene just looked like a painting of a haughty child being spoiled by his big sisters.

In the church's office.

Chastille was chewing on some bread for breakfast while sitting at her desk.

"Huh? A gathering of elders?" Barbatos asked as he popped out of the shadows with a hunk of meat in his hands. He had an unhealthy looking face with large shadows around his eyes, which were really no different from usual even though Nephteros had cured them just the other day, and several amulets dangling down from his neck. Barbatos ruffled his unkempt hair as he looked up suspiciously at Chastille, who cleared her throat out with a cough.

"It's an important conference where all the races of the continent gather. Please don't cause any trouble, okay? Also, don't speak while you're eating. It's rude."

"Oh, come on! What kind of crap do you expect me to pull, exactly? I've been protecting you like a gentleman this whole time, so at least have a little faith!"

"I can tell that you'd try to capture any rare species you see, you know?"

"Huh? Well, yeah, I'm a sorcerer. Why wouldn't I do that?"

Chastille let out a sigh as her headache set in. This man was Zagan's undesirable friend, an ex-Archdemon candidate, and also the sorcerer who was assigned to be her escort. He couldn't be trusted, but he was rather reliable as well.

"I'm telling you not to do that. Listen, I'm not just going on behalf of the church. They chose me to represent all humans."

"Yeah yeah, don't worry. Your babysitter will follow you anywhere."

Barbatos was capable of traversing any distance in an instant. That was a fairly useful skill in practice, but it also meant she could never shake him.

He wasn't a bad person at heart... No, he was a villain who was rotten to the core, but on rare occasions, he showed a soft side. However, that didn't change the fact that he was normally an irredeemable individual. And just as Barbatos began cackling, a shortsword stabbed into the floor right in front of his eyes.

"The hell!?"

"Oh, sorry. My hand slipped. Next time I'll make sure to bring it down on your neck."

"Apologize properly, dammit!"

The one who taunted him without an ounce of timidness in her voice was Kuroka. She entered the room with a letter in hand, and was accompanied by Nephteros and an Angelic Knight. As always, Kuroka carried two shortswords. Though at this particular moment, one was in the ground in front of Barbatos and the other was at the ready to stab him in the face.

"You bitch... What the hell do you think you're doing!?"

"Uh, I was just thinking of doing a little cleaning...?" Kuroka replied. Then, she turned her vacant eyes toward him with a cold gaze and cocked her head to the side before saying, "Please watch your mouth, Mister Sorcerer. If not for Lady Chastille, I would cut off your head here and now."

"You got some grudge against sorcerers or what?"

"I'll never forgive them for stealing my friends, family, and the light in my eyes..."

"Crap, this one's serious..." Barbatos muttered as he shut his mouth. Kuroka was on friendly terms with Zagan, who settled things between her and Chastille, but that didn't mean she had suddenly forgiven all sorcerers. In fact, she was more wary of them than ever because Chastille seemed to trust them so blindly.

"Kuroka, getting angry at him each and every time will only tire you out," Nephteros said in exasperation.

"...You've narrowly escaped death, Mister Sorcerer. Still, don't just assume you'll make it out safely next time, okay?" Kuroka said in a dry tone as she stomped on the end of the scabbard at her feet and skillfully sheathed her swords in mid-air.

"Bring it on, bitch! Did you fucking forget I turned the tables on you last time!?"

"Geez… Cut it out, Barbatos. You said you were coming to the gathering of elders, right? You should at least go prepare for the journey," Chastille plainly stated.

"Wait, you're not gonna tell me to stay behind?" Barbatos asked as he stared at her in wonder.

"You'll just follow me anyway, right? In that case, stand by my side."

"…O-Okay," Barbatos hesitantly responded as if he was unsure how to react. And just like that, he sank into the shadows and disappeared.

Kuroka let out a 'hmph' as she gazed at his shadow with her tails standing straight on end, but Barbatos had left, so there was no one left there to react to her. Chastille grew impatient as she watched her do that and decided to call out to her.

"He's just teasing me, Kuroka. You don't have to pay any serious attention to him."

"Lady Chastille, I'm fully aware that it's impolite of me to say this, but that man is a monster. He's a villain who's rotten down to his very core. I won't claim that all sorcerers are evil, but he definitely is. An Archangel like you shouldn't be associating yourself with him."

What to do? I can't deny any of that, but… Chastille was stumped by Kuroka's sound argument. Luckily, Nephteros decided to throw her a lifeline.

"That's what makes him the perfect bodyguard. Barbatos is a greedy, selfish sorcerer, so he'll never betray you as long as you pay him well."

"That's certainly another way of looking at it, but…" Kuroka mumbled in discontent as Nephteros shook her head with her silver hair swaying in the air.

"Wouldn't that guy probably protect Chastille for free?"

"Huh…? Why do you think he would do that?" Kuroka asked as both she and Chastille cocked their heads to the side. Then, Nephteros replied to her question in a matter-of-fact tone.

"I mean, isn't he in love with you?"

Loaf…? Lobe? No, loan…? Maybe lode…? Chastille was unable to comprehend what she just heard. And after a while, vocabulary that made no sense at all in context went through her brain.

"I'm telling you he's head over heels for you," Nephteros piled on those words in an attempt to stem Chastille's stalling.

"AWEGQWERGQQQ!?" Chastille blurted out some incoherent sounds, then said, "Wh-Wh-Wh-Wh-Wh-Wh-Wh-What are you saying!?"

"What indeed, Miss Nephteros! Love? Please. If he does feel that way, then he's more like a disgusting stalker!"

"N-No, you don't need to go that far…" Chastille remarked, still completely shocked.

"Am I wrong?" Nephteros said, knitting her brows.

"You're completely wrong! I mean, it's Barbatos!"

"What's that supposed to mean…?" Nephteros replied in astonishment. Then, she stated, "That guy's voice goes up half an octave whenever he's talking to you. Plus, he even started calling you by your name recently. And above all else, he's always in good humor when you two speak."

"Um, uh, th-there's no way…" Chastille muttered, looking shaken as the truth dawned on her.

Now that I think about it, he did jump in and sacrifice himself to save me back when Kuroka first attacked… A sorcerer who only cared about getting paid wouldn't have put their life on the line. And yet, Barbatos jumped in to act as her shield and allowed himself to be cut and stabbed numerous times. Chastille knew full well that he wasn't a man who would do such a thing, so…

"Besides, when you told him to stand by your side, his ears turned red. Doesn't that mean he's in love?" Nephteros delivered her finishing blow in a calm, steady manner.

"S-Stop! Please just leave it at that! I-If you say any more, I won't even know how to face him…" Chastilled mumbled in an embarrassed tone.

"Our best course of action is to finish him off, right? Don't worry, thanks to my time with Azazel, I'm an expert."

"Stop right there!" Nephteros yelled as she grabbed the nape of Kuroka's neck, stopping her from leaving to carry out her heinous plot.

"You want definitive proof that he won't betray us, right? Well, now you have it. Why would he ever betray the woman he loves?"

"Um, well, that's a good point, but…"

That Barbatos… with me? Chastille thought the idea impossible, but for some reason it was also hard for her to completely deny it. And while she agonized over those feelings, the Angelic Knight next to Nephteros formed a strained smile.

"Please stop, Lady Nephteros. Most women don't enjoy talking about their love lives in public."

"Is that so?"

"Yes. Do you not have any experience with it yourself?"

"I don't. After all, I'm nowhere near as old as I look," Nephteros said as she shrugged her shoulders. In truth, it hadn't even been a full year since she was created. She was terribly hurt by the fact that she was just Nephy's clone, and was still worried about it, but oddly enough, Chastille couldn't sense even a hint of agony in her voice.

It seems she's at a point where she's fine speaking about it now... Chastille was basically praying that was true, as nothing could have made her happier.

"I'm sure you'll eventually meet a man who treasures you more than anything else in the world, Lady Nephteros," the Angelic Knight said in a charmed manner.

"I wonder if there's anyone out there with such bad taste..."

"There definitely is. In fact, I guarantee it."

She may be observant, but she's completely clueless when it comes to herself... This particular Angelic Knight, Richard, was part of the patrol that bumped into Nephteros when she was being attacked by the chimera. After recovering from his wounds, he kept trying to interact with her as much as possible, which made it clear he was in love with Nephteros.

"...Sir Richard, please hang in there," Kuroka said as she let out a long sigh. Her ears practically flopped down in disappointment as she watched them interact. Richard, however, merely formed a strained smile in response.

Let's just not think about Barbatos' matter for now. I'm sure it's just Nephteros' imagination... Chastille thought as she finally got her mind and breathing in order.

Unfortunately, a new question suddenly popped into her to mind and threw her into disarray once more. *What do I even think of Barbatos...?*

It hadn't even been a week since she realized she was in love with Zagan, so Chastille found herself unable to answer that question.

"Stop right here, Foll!" Zagan yelled at Foll as she tugged him through Kianoides. Incidentally, because they could find no clothes that fit Zagan, he simply lopped off the pieces of his usual robes to make them fit, then tied the rest together.

"What's wrong?" Foll asked as she looked back at him and curiously tilted her head.

"What's wrong? Do you even need to ask? Why are we going to this shop of all places!?"

They were currently in front of their usual clothing shop. Zagan used it often, and the clerk there was someone he was on good terms with, but…

"You bought my clothes here. They have stuff for boys, too. It's okay."

"…You don't get it. If Manuela sees me like this, I'm doomed."

"Huh? But Nephy said she was a nice person. You shouldn't be in any danger."

That wasn't a lie or anything, but Manuela also didn't have much in the way of self-control. Unfortunately, the two of them caused quite a commotion right outside the shop, which obviously attracted attention.

"What's with all this noise?"

The door opened with a clank, and out came the avian clerk with green wings, Manuela. This woman was one of Nephy's best friends, which meant Zagan held her in high esteem, but… she often turned into quite the nuisance when it came to clothing people.

Wait, I've only ever seen her toy with girls. Maybe she doesn't have any interest in boys... Plus, there was also the chance that she didn't dare fool around with him because he was an Archdemon. Still, Zagan raised his guard just in case as Foll stepped up to her.

"We're here to buy clothes."

"Huh? Hm...? Um, I don't think it's possible, but... are you Foll?" Manuela knit her brows as she asked that question.

"I am," Foll responded. And at that point, she finally remembered what she looked like, so she spread out her arms and spun on the spot.

"I got bigger," Foll explained as the cloth around her chest burst open once more. Zagan had to fix her clothes in an instant to keep her from being fully exposed.

"I keep telling you not to make any sudden movements..." Zagan muttered, drawing Manuela's attention to him.

"Um, sooo, who's this kid?"

"Zagan."

"Pffft," Manuela snorted before bursting into laughter and saying, "How!? He's so cute! How did you end up so amus... so deligh... joyful? Hmm... Well, whatever. You're all amusicute now, Zagan!"

"Don't just make up words!" Zagan roared as he wondered why she gave up on finding the proper word so easily.

"Geheheh, well, let me hear all the juicy details inside. We've got two paying customers here!" Manuela scooped Zagan into her arms and walked him into the shop as he was lost in thought.

Oh, I see. It had nothing to do with me being an Archdemon. Manuela's just not interested in adults... As he was dragged inside, he spotted another familiar face.

"Welcome!"

The girl with fluffy white ears who welcomed them with a smile was a vulpin. Her "uniform" was a one-piece dress that looked similar to what Nephy wore. The main differences were the frilly lace all over the dress and the headband that fit snugly between her ears.

"Kuu? Why the hell are you here?" Zagan asked.

"Hm? Do you know me? Well, even if you do, you should respect your elders. Otherwise, this scary lady might just treat you like a toy!" Kuu's fluffy ears quivered about in an annoyed manner as she said that. It seemed like she didn't notice that the child in front of her was Zagan.

Maybe it's better this way... Acting like an innocent child seemed preferable to having more people know about his situation. And so, he bit down on his lips and formed a faint smile.

"S-Sorry, Miss Kuu. I saw you at the church before, so I just blurted that out without thinking," Zagan claimed. Then, a loud thud resounded from behind him, and when he turned around, he spotted Manuela rolling around the ground with her hands on her stomach.

Fuck! I'll remember this... Even if she was Nephy's friend, she really was going too far. The way she behaved reminded Zagan of Gremory, which made a shiver run down his spine. And having interpreted the expression on Zagan's face as one of regret, Kuu pat his head to comfort him.

"Is that so? Heehee, it's good that you apologized right away... Oh, but you should really work on that smile of yours. It looked just like Mister Zagan's does when he's picking a fight."

Does she remember what happened when Bifrons took control of her body? Zagan's face stiffened as soon as he heard her say that. Kuu went through a lot when Bifrons manipulated her, which was why Zagan asked Orias to wipe her memories. Though, looking back on it, he didn't recall her actually accepting his request.

Hm, it seems like I also suck at smiling... Zagan thought of the way Nephy pulled at her own cheeks to practice. And as he did, he realized that he had to put in the same amount of effort since he was her groom. That was why he pulled at his own cheeks. He'd assumed his facial muscles were still stiff, but it seemed like turning into a child had made them all stretchy. He kept stretching them over and over, and eventually, someone hugged him from behind.

"What are you doing?" Zagan asked. He was confused about why Foll was hugging him so tightly.

"Cute."

"Huh? Who're you calling cute!?" Zagan protested. However, that didn't deter Foll from rubbing her cheek against his. And when he tried to tear himself away, Kuu came over and pet his head once more.

"Oh, boys really hate it when you call them cute, don't they? But you know, it's really not that bad because it makes us want to hug you!"

"Grrr..." Zagan growled in annoyance. Though, thinking back, he recalled that Foll constantly hugged Nephy and called her cute when she was turned into a child. Perhaps that meant she just had a habit of hugging cute things.

"Hm… You know, you kind of look like Mister Zagan. You're all dressed up like a sorcerer, too… Are you related to him?" Kuu asked as she cocked her head to the side.

"W-Well…" Zagan was rendered silent as he tried to think up an excuse.

"Huh? What do you mean? Zagan is Zaghamph," Foll tried to expose his secret despite her hesitation, but luckily, Manuela came in and silenced her by covering up her mouth.

"This child is Zagan's distant relative, Dagan. Oh, and this pretty lady here is his older sister, Farah. They're Zagan's guests, so mind your manners around them, alright Kuu?" Manuela said in an attempt to help Zagan hide his identity. Then, she silently whispered into Foll's ear and said, "Play along, okay?"

In an unusual turn, Foll was quick on the uptake, so she simply bobbed her head up and down in response.

"By the way, who exactly is this 'scary lady' who treats children like toys?" Manuela asked Kuu as she turned to her.

"Huh? What are you talking about? You must be confused! I just said that bad kids should be punished!" Kuu exclaimed as she straightened her back with a snap.

Oh, I see. Manuela must already treat her like a toy… Zagan felt bad for her.

"So Dagan is Mister Zagan's relative? I wonder if you'll look like him when you grow up? Oh, in that case, you should learn to be nice to girls before it's too late!"

She really does remember everything, doesn't she? Zagan mercilessly thrust his arm right through her heart during their last meeting. Even if her memories were erased, that pain probably remained fresh in her mind. And upon realizing that, Zagan was overcome by a sense of guilt.

"Um, Zagan seemed worried about that as well, and he said he wouldn't do such mean things again. So, um, please relax. You won't have any more painful memories. He won't allow it."

Zagan was giving her his best attempt at an apology, but for some reason, Kuu's face was turning red as she took in his words.

"Hnnngh… Oh, what's this feeling? Th-This is bad, Kuu. He's just a kid," Kuu mumbled those words as she gripped her chest, then walked away while fanning herself.

Well, I guess I should've known that comforting words weren't going to be enough… In the end, he had probably just made her remember a painful memory instead of helping her get over it, and knowing that made Zagan droop his shoulders in disappointment.

"Zagan, you shouldn't be too kind to people in your current form," Manuela said as she reached her wit's end.

"You think I was being kind? Please, I was just speaking my mind," Zagan replied.

"Uh… I mean, that'd be fine if you were your normal self, but when you're all tiny there's something about it that seems oddly charming… Even I find it hard to resist you right now…"

"Ch-Charming…?" Zagan stuttered in a confused tone. Honestly, he kind of understood what she meant, but the concept also confused him, so he decided to save thinking about it for later.

Hold on, isn't she really similar to that granny…? He prayed that Gremory and Manuela would never meet, lest his life be ruined.

"I'll be careful…" Zagan obediently answered, which made Manuela face break out into a broad grin.

"Alright, time to get you changed!"

"No, I can pick out my own clothes… Hey, are you listening? Wait, what are you holding? Stop! Don't get any closer!" Zagan desperately screamed for Manuela to stop as she walked over to him with a skirt and one-piece dress in her hands.

"Fufufu, you're a lot cuter when you're shy... Foll, hold him in place so we can get this over with."

"Oh, okay," Foll replied. Her body may have grown, but she was still the same innocent girl at heart, so she trusted Manuela wholeheartedly.

"Stop, let me go... NOOOOOOOOOOOOOOOO!"

Several minutes later, Zagan was covered in frills and lace like some little princess.

How dare she do this to me... Usually, Zagan didn't go anywhere near the changing room, so he was unaware that entering it was the same as falling into the pits of hell.

"Hnnngh! My eyes definitely weren't wrong! You really do have potential! Be more confident in yourself!"

"What confidence...? Don't screw with me..." Zagan meekly muttered that, seemingly having lost his will to fight her.

"Manuela, these are girl's clothes. No more pranks," Foll said as she tilted her head to the side in confusion. Then, she puffed out her cheeks, and contrary to Zagan's expectations, Manuela's eyes sparkled.

"Wow, I should've known. You may have grown, but you still look adorable... Look, see Zagan right now? Don't those clothes look good on him?"

"They do, but I can tell he doesn't like them, so stop," Foll demanded. Zagan was shocked that his own daughter was sticking up for him.

"Hm, I guess you're right. Wow, you've become a proper big sister, Foll. I'm proud of you," Manuela said as she wiped her eyes, which seemed to be on the verge of leaking proud tears.

"Big sister...! Yeah, I'm... his big sister," Foll said as she puffed out her chest with flushed cheeks.

That part of her is still childish, but whatever... Zagan decided not to say anything because he found her actions cute.

"Well, I guess that's enough playing around. It was fun, but now it's time to pick out some real clothes," Manuela said as she squeezed down on Zagan's shoulders. Then, she spun him around on the spot once. And just as he started to wonder what she was doing, his frilly outfit was replaced by a dashing suit that came complete with a puff tie. He was wearing rather tight clothes that made him look like an uppity noble, which would hold him back in a fight, but it did make him look good.

I actually wanted her to get me something like this for my date with Nephy... Zagan had planned to ask for her help with that earlier, but there was no point now. After all, he wasn't even sure if he would return to his normal form anytime soon.

Foll stood and clapped with sparkles in her eyes as she watched Manuela change his clothes in an instant.

"You're amazing."

"Fufufu, aren't I? Aren't I? Go on, praise me more!" Manuela exclaimed. Her skills were rather impressive, but the fact that she was starting to act more impudent rubbed Zagan the wrong way.

"...Are you a sorcerer?" Zagan asked, his confusion evident due to the look on his face.

"I am simply the clerk of a clothing store. Nothing more, and nothing less. More importantly, what do you think of Foll's clothes?"

He hadn't even noticed that she had dressed her, so he turned to her to take in the new sight. Foll was wearing a one-piece dress that had an elegant piece of armor over it. Both parts matched and made her look beautiful, so Zagan thought it was a good choice.

"It's a little tight, but also easy to move around in. Still, I don't need armor. This thing'll just get in the way," Foll explained as she did a little twirl on the spot. Sure, Foll was young, but since she was a dragon, her body was still protected by her scales. They weren't visible in her human form, but they still projected a sort of magical barrier that made all normal weapons and sorcery useless.

"That's not it, Foll. Your breasts are really heavy now, right?" Manuela asked as she shook her head at Foll's previous statement.

"How do you know?" Foll replied as she stared back at her in wonder.

"I can tell just by looking. You see, they start to hurt your shoulders when they're that big, but wearing a breastplate will lighten the load. Just think of it as underwear you have on over your clothes," Manuela said as she thoroughly explained her reasoning.

"I see. You're amazing," Foll responded, voicing her honest opinion.

However, for some reason, all that talk of underwear had Zagan blushing. *Wait, why do I find that so embarrassing?*

He could understand blushing if they were talking about Nephy's underwear, but this was his daughter. No matter how big she got, he would never see her as anything else.

Is my mind being influenced by my new body? When Nephy turned into a child, her mind also started to degrade to match her age. Perhaps he was experiencing similar symptoms. It seemed he didn't have much time, so Zagan resolved to take action immediately. And just then, the door to the shop swung open.

"Welcome! Oh, hi there, Miss Gremory!" Kuu, who had been watching them from from a far off corner, reacted to the intruder right away.

"Hello. Oh my, your face has quite the lovely look on it, doesn't it?"

"I don't really get what you mean, but thanks!"

And the one to show up, was Gremory.

Huh? Kuu knows Gremory?

Gremory casually raised her hand and greeted Kuu, then immediately looked over to Zagan. However, instead of walking up to him, she stopped right in front of Manuela.

"Welcome, Comrade Gremory."

"Good work, Comrade Manuela."

This town is doomed... Zagan was left speechless as he watched the two of them exchange salutes.

Judging from their use of the term comrade, these two were already well beyond the realm of just acquaintances. The two who should never have met were already conspiring together. And while Zagan turned pale at that reality, Gremory finally addressed him.

"I thought you'd come here. Looks like you finished changing without any problems. Well, I'm sure you'll be happy to learn I managed to get in contact with my teacher."

"Oh, uh, good job..." Zagan said that and nodded as his expression began to cloud over.

"Come now, it's not like you to look depressed. Don't worry, you have both me and my teacher on your side, so I'm certain you'll return to normal in no time," Gremory claimed as she puffed out her chest proudly.

After that, Zagan and Foll followed Gremory out of the shop. And sure enough, what awaited them was—

"I am truly sorry for all the trouble my foolish disciple has caused you." Orias said that, bowed deeply, and apologized to Zagan as soon as they met. As usual, she was wearing a hood that covered most of her face and a baggy robe to hide her high elf nature. In fact, her, Nephy, and Nephteros were likely the only living high elves in existence. And she also happened to be Gremory's teacher, which meant she could easily manipulate her own physical age. However, the features of her face that could be discerned were those of an old woman, and her voice was also hoarse. Incidentally, Gremory had a large lump on her head and was weeping. The moment they met, Orias had brought her fist down upon her.

"Um, no. This is due to my own carelessness, so I wouldn't hold her entirely responsible…"

"Do not spoil her. There's the matter of what happened at the hidden village, too. Back then, she was using sorcery to watch you run around like a headless chicken."

"Alright. Rake her over the coals all you want," Zagan said as his feelings of sympathy for her completely vanished.

"My liege, I think it would be fine to treat me just a little more kindly…"

"Ask for that after you reflect on your actions."

"Are you telling me that she did other things as well?" Orias chimed in.

Being glared at by two Archdemons was more than enough to make Gremory kneel in silence.

"I feel like I've been kneeling since this morning…" Gremory mumbled, clearly unhappy.

"It seems you've heard the gist of things from Gremory, but I ended up like this after we failed in casting some sorcery. I'm looking for a way to reverse this transformation, so do you have any ideas? I intend to pay you back in a suitable manner, of course," Zagan said as he turned to face Orias. Then, he bowed down respectfully to her, and Orias simply shrugged her shoulders.

"There's no need for you to act so distant. I already owe you a great debt. You brought my daughter happiness, which is something I can never hope to repay," Orias stated before turning to Foll and saying, "And this one is the dragon girl, right? I've heard she's your adopted daughter?"

"Valefor. You can call me Foll."

"Well, in that case, you may call me Granny."

"Got it. Granny," Foll replied with a completely serious expression on her face, which made Orias scratch the tip of her nose in a troubled manner.

"…Sorry. I meant that in jest."

This person is always apologizing, isn't she? Zagan formed a bitter smile as he mulled over her joke. It may have been Orias' attempt to liven up the mood, but she seemed to have failed.

"You're Nephy's mommy, so it's not strange for you to be my granny," Foll claimed as she cocked her head to the side in confusion. Orias gaped in surprise upon hearing that, then smiled pleasantly.

"Nephy has quite the straightforward daughter, I see," Orias said that, then cast her gaze over to Zagan and continued, "Now then, let me have a look. Show me your right hands," Orias demanded. Then, Zagan and Foll held them out, and the Sigil of the Archdemon appeared on both of them.

"Hm… It seems to be the same sigil."

"What does that mean?" Zagan inquired. Orias, however, simply touched the sigil without answering, and observed it for a while before letting out a groan.

"This looks to be quite a troublesome situation. This is my first time seeing such a complicated curse."

"Is it hard for even you to dispel it?"

"…You're correct. Sorry," Orias apologized, bowing her head deeply all the while.

"Please raise your head. This is nothing for you to apologize about," Zagan barked back, seemingly flustered.

"For the time being, I'll let you in on everything I can discern. First off, Zagan, your sigil has lost most of its power. At this point, even if I were to suppress its power with mine, it would likely only have an effect on you," Orias claimed as she looked back up at Zagan apologetically. Foll also had a sigil now, but the main part of it was still Zagan's, which meant the outward flow of power had no effect on Foll.

"Next up, Foll. I'm sure you're a child of an exceptional bloodline even among dragons. The power within you is from the age of myths. In other words, it is quite literally godlike. It's so vast that I'm certain you could easily challenge most of the current Archdemons."

"I see…" Zagan muttered, then said, "Foll is the daughter of Wise Dragon Orobas, who was said to have lived through the age of myths, so that makes sense."

In an unusual turn, Orias' eyes shot wide open in shock upon hearing that.

"That's… quite the hapless fate. It almost makes me want to believe in destiny."

"What do you mean?" Zagan inquired.

"Marchosias was Wise Dragon Orobas' sworn friend," Orias stated as she turned to Foll with a gentle look in her eyes. Foll, on the other hand, audibly gulped upon hearing that.

"Somehow, it feels nostalgic."

That was what Foll had said when Zagan first brought her to Archdemon Palace. That, plus the fact that Archdemon Palace was filled with mechanisms that utilized dragon spells, made Zagan wonder if Archdemon Marchosias' power was something granted to him by Orobas.

"Is this all a coincidence...?" Zagan mumbled.

"I wonder... Marchosias' successor somehow ended up adopting Orobas' daughter... Makes you wonder if this is all a part of someone's master plan, doesn't it?" Orias asked, then once more turned toward Foll and said, "Going back to what we were talking about before. Foll, your power is something that should have unraveled slowly over a long period of time. The current situation was brought about by trying to artificially remove that limit. It's almost as if all the water within an infinite well burst out at once and flooded its surroundings."

"It's... all my fault..." Foll cast her gaze downward, blaming herself for all of Zagan's misfortune.

"No. That's simply hindsight. If your power truly ran wild, then Zagan and my foolish disciple would be dead already. That's why you should consider yourself lucky and learn from it," Orias claimed. Her words were both kind and strict, which made Foll return a firm nod in response.

That's essentially what I should have told her... He could have used his change in form as an excuse, but Zagan knew that would be the same as lying to himself. Frankly, the whole matter just made him realize how inexperienced he still was.

"Now then, as I explained, you're currently like the flowing current from a broken dam. The key to it is the Sigil of the Archdemon, but that was washed away as well. To stop the flow, you need to either rebuild the dam or find the key. Both are extremely difficult tasks, but they are your only options," Orias spoke of their path forward in a gentle tone. Her answer was quite vague, but Zagan felt like he grasped the full picture of the curse thanks to it.

In that case, if we forcefully cut off the path we created, Foll would be in more danger than me... If they took away the source of water behind the broken dam, the lake would dry up.

"Hm, perhaps this situation was brought about by your sigil, Zagan."

"What do you mean?" Zagan asked. However, instead of answering immediately, Orias held out her right hand.

"This is my sigil. Can you tell that its shape is a little different from yours?" Orias inquired.

"Yeah," Zagan responded. It was something Zagan vaguely realized when he saw Bifrons' sigil. At a glance, they looked identical, but Zagan and Orias' sigils differed slightly in their minute details.

"I've discovered something similar to these. Namely, the Sacred Swords of the church. Whatever's carved on them appears to also be in Celestian."

"That's correct. You could say that these Sigils of the Archdemon are a type of circuit created with Celestian. Though, it may be more accurate to call it a cipher. Unfortunately, reproducing anything similar would prove difficult even for me," Orias replied. Zagan opened his eyes wide upon hearing that it was such an advanced technique that even an Archdemon would find it hard to reproduce.

"Nevertheless, I killed some time unraveling this cipher. After all, time was the one thing I had in abundance."

"And what does it say…?"

"It's nothing all that impressive. Seal, power, connect, god, evil. Something along those lines. Well, those are about the only words with meaning, anyway. The others are all things I can't even understand. However…" Orias paused for a moment there, and stared right into Zagan's eyes before saying, "Within this sigil, there is a word that signifies the right hand."

"Right hand…?" Zagan mumbled, seemingly confused. As far as he knew, all the Sigils of the Archdemon were located on the right hands of those who possessed them. Did that have some kind of meaning to it?

"Hm… I've already considered that it may be because the sigils always appear on a person's right hand. However, that seems unrelated," Orias said that, then pointed to Zagan's sigil and continued, "The part of my sigil that signifies the right hand has been replaced by something that means heart on yours."

Zagan's eyes shot open, and Orias gave him a silent nod.

"To sorcerers, the heart is not merely the cornerstone of life, but also the furnace that gives birth to an enormous amount of mana. In other words, there is a high probability that your sigil produces the most mana among the thirteen. At any rate, it was Eldest's sigil."

That was a rather shocking revelation, but one other point was on Zagan's mind.

The heart, the right hand… Each is a piece of a body. In that case, Bifrons' sigil likely symbolized some other part of the body. And that made Zagan realize…

"In other words, the Sigils of the Archdemon really do seal away the body of the Demon Lord…" Zagan muttered in a grave tone. That meant Zagan's sigil contained the Demon Lord's heart, which was like an infinite furnace of mana. It meant that Bifrons' conjecture was correct. However, Orias let out a dubious voice.

"Demon Lord...? Oh, is that how you refer to it? I see. It's easy enough to understand."

Now that I think about it, only Bifrons called it the Demon Lord...

"Well, what do you call it?"

"Me? Hm, I've never actually given it a name. There was never any need. Oh, but let's see..." Orias trailed off, then spoke in a somewhat nostalgic tone, "Marchosias called it... the Primordial Archdemon."

Zagan couldn't tell what that signified. However, it matched the sigil's name at least. After all, it was the Sigil of the Archdemon, not the Sigil of the Demon Lord.

Still, I feel like all our assumptions are way off base... Unfortunately, Zagan was far too inexperienced to figure out how. An Archdemon of Bifrons' level spent hundreds of years studying it just to create celestial mysticism, so a newcomer like Zagan had a long way to go before he could get to the heart of the matter. And as those talks came to an end, Orias finally relaxed.

"Well then, I'll try to search for a way to undo this curse, but don't expect too much. A mere high elf can't hope to compare to the power of legends."

"No, you've been a huge help already. Allow me to offer you my thanks."

After Zagan humbly offered his gratitude, Orias continued on quietly.

"Also, Zagan, do you know about Liucaon? The island nation, I mean."

"Yeah. In fact, I got to know someone from there recently."

"I see. How fortuitous. This is the last piece of advice I can give you. Try relying on Liucaon. There are several secrets that remain there that have been lost to us for quite some time. The tools they use for rituals, which are called Holy Treasures, resemble Sacred Swords. Perhaps an ancient power resides there that can do something to combat this curse."

Zagan had heard that powers different from sorcery existed in Liucaon, and Gremory had even listed that as one of their possible choices, so that seemed like a good lead.

It's better than just sitting on my thumbs, anyway...

"Do you know of the Continental Interracial Elders Conference?"

"Of course. I am one of the last remaining elves, so I've at least heard the name."

"Would people from Liucaon attend?" Zagan asked.

"Definitely. They're one of the most important participants," Orias replied.

"Actually, I was invited too. I'm not sure who exactly will attend, but I'm thinking of making an appearance."

"What!? Why didn't you tell me!? Just thinking of all the love power from all the races gathering makes me drool..." Gremory had a visceral reaction upon hearing that.

"You must help me search for a way to undo the curse, you thoughtless fool," Orias cut Gremory's excitation off in a cold tone.

"P-Please let me off for now! I promise to help once I get back from the conference, so just give me one free night!"

"Have you been sincere enough with me that I would allow such a thing?"

"You demooooooon!"

Zagan and Foll returned to the castle, leaving the screaming Gremory behind with her mentor.

"Pheeew, really, thank goodness. Mister Archdemon didn't seem to, like, care about that conference at all," Selphy said, seemingly in high spirits as she was stirring a pot of soup in the kitchen. She was in such a good mood that she even began humming. And as she did, her boss, who was preparing the main dish behind her, let out a groan.

"Fool. My liege is unable to participate in that trifle because he is far too busy, but do you think you can use that as a reason to exempt yourself?"

"Um, you mean, like, a representative or someone might have to go, so don't start celebrating? It's totally fine. Like I said, Mister Archdemon really didn't seem to care. Plus, if he went, everyone would be all scared, so, like, this works out better!"

Selphy spoke to the rather frightening man in a casual manner. Raphael's face and conduct were terrifying, but a simple conversation was enough to realize he was a good man at heart. In fact, it could be said that he was the kindest person Selphy had met. Well, aside from Nephy, anyway.

He spends a lot of time training me on the job, and praises me if I do well, too... He was always upright and honest, though not many people noticed due to his manner of speech. It was most unfortunate that his phrasing and choice of vocabulary was awkward and created misunderstandings.

That part of him is a little like my friend from back home, though... Even Selphy had at least one person she could call a friend. She hadn't spoken to her since fleeing her hometown, but her childhood friend was someone who spoke and acted much like Raphael. Also, she let Selphy sing all she wanted.

"Hmph… It seems you've also come to a damn understanding of the wideness of my liege's bosom. He possesses genuine ambitions, so he has thorough knowledge of techniques that can both destroy and tame the ignorant masses," Raphael said as a sneer rose to his face.

"Genuine ambitions… Oh, like, about Miss Nephy? Well, you've got a point there. Seeing them flirt, like, all day really makes him seem less scary."

This butler was a perfect fit for that Archdemon, in that both of them acted in baffling ways. The Archdemon was relatively easy to read, though. Especially when it came to the woman he loved. The way he ran about in confusion when it came to speaking to Nephy didn't suit the aura of terror and majesty that generally surrounded Archdemons. And in those times, he seemed like just an ordinary clumsy boy.

Still, he can, like, turn a whole boat into dust with a single punch… Basically, he could jokingly poke Selphy's head and send her off to the afterlife. And in that respect, he truly was an Archdemon. Though, if all the other Archdemons were people like Zagan, the world probably would've been a far more peaceful place.

"Hey! Pay some damn attention!" Raphael roared at Selphy as she got lost in thought. And when she looked up, she saw that the butler was aiming a fierce glare at her.

"Eeek, did you find out I was thinking of having a little taste?"

"You'll ruin it. Get the pot off the fire."

"Oh, okaaay… Hm, how's it taste? Wouldn't it, like, be better if it was a lil' sweeter?" Selphy said that, then immediately took a wet towel and brought the pot down from the fire. After pouring some of the soup into a small dish and tasting it, she cocked her head to the side. Raphael followed suit and tasted the soup as well, but shook his head instead.

111

"No, this is good. The seasoning on the main dish is rather strong, so it will pair well with the taste of this soup. You've performed admirably."

"Yaaay! Mister Raphael praised me!" Selphy exclaimed as she threw her hands into the air in celebration. And at that exact moment, a tall therianthrope stalked into the kitchen.

"I'm sorry to disturb you. My hands are free right now, so is there anything I can help with?"

This therianthrope with a bushy mane and the face of a lion was Kimaris. Like Gremory, he was Zagan's trusted retainer. In fact, the two of them were so powerful that they competed for the top spot among Zagan's followers. However, despite that, he was so kind that he even dropped by to help in the kitchen when he had free time.

"Indeed. You've come at a good time. We've just about finished here. Grab enough plates for everyone," Raphael wasted no time and immediately barked out his orders.

"Alright. Oh, Miss Selphy, those plates must be heavy, so allow me to handle them."

"Thanks, Mister Kimaris. Mister Raphael even praised my soup today, so I'm, like, totally confident about the taste!"

"I'll look forward to it, then," Kimaris said, then tilted his head to the side and asked, "What shall we do about Sir Zagan and Foll's portions? I believe they're out at the moment."

"I haven't been informed of when they'll return, but we should prepare for them anyway."

Kimaris quietly accepted the butler's orders, but then curiosity overcame him.

"...By the way, did something happen today? I haven't seen Miss Gremory around either."

"Hm… I'm certain my liege would have informed you directly himself, but a little problem occurred. Gremory is accompanying him on his hunt for a solution."

"…What did Miss Gremory do this time?" Kimaris asked as he began scratching his head.

"Hey now, it's not like the culprit is necessarily Miss Gremory!"

Other sorcerers treated Gremory like a troublesome granny, but Selphy thought she was a good person. She often gave Selphy candy, and would gaze at her with a broad grin. Yet, Kimaris, who was supposed to be her closest friend, made a stern expression as he shook his head.

"No, if it wasn't her fault, Sir Zagan would have asked for my help as well. The fact that he didn't must mean he doesn't want me to feel guilty about Miss Gremory's mistake. Though, I suppose it's also possible that he simply did not have the time to tell me," Kimaris said that, then paused and added, "Also, Lady Nephy scolded Miss Gremory yesterday. She seemed rather angry, so I'm certain it was her fault."

"…Oh." Selphy muttered. She couldn't refute that last point at all. The very idea of Nephy getting angry seemed impossible, so there had to have been a good reason for it to happen.

"Now that I think of it, Sir Raphael, did you manage to ask Sir Zagan about the matter we discussed?" Kimaris asked as he suddenly turned to look at Raphael.

"Urgh… No, he's been quite busy, so I haven't had the time," Raphael responded in an extremely vague way, which Selphy found quite strange.

"Huh? Did something happen?"

"It's nothing important. It has nothing to do with you."

"Aww, come on! Aren't we kitchen pals!? Leaving me out is, like, really mean! Please tell me!" Selphy threw a tantrum, but for some reason it was Kimaris who looked apologetic.

"My apologies, Sir Raphael. I should have been more careful…"

"It's fine. It's not actually something that needs hiding," Raphael said that, then turned to Selphy and explained, "I've been having some strange dreams lately. They are likely the memories of a certain dragon."

"By dragon, you mean someone like Foll? Why would a human see those?"

"Due to certain special circumstances, I have dragon blood flowing through me… Anyway, since the visions are so frequent, I feel like that dragon is trying to tell me something."

"I see. So that's why the little lady is so attached to you, Mister Raphael!" Selphy nodded to herself, clearly pleased about whatever strange deduction she made.

"…" Raphael and Kimaris both looked at Selphy like they were facing a dumb brat.

"Well, they're just dreams. It's fine not to trouble my liege with such minor matters when he's already in a bind."

"No, wait. If it's about dreams, then my friend Lilith is, like, kind of an expert," Selphy spoke those words in a worried tone. She felt Raphael may collapse if he carried that burden all on his own.

"I know this may sound rude, but aren't sirens more affiliated with an eternal slumber of sorts?"

"Lilith is a succubus. She can, like, go into people's dreams and play pranks on them. Sometimes, when I took a nap, she made me see a dream where I was killed by some sorcerers. Luckily, when I woke up, my big sis would totally comfort me!"

"Are you certain you didn't see those dreams after getting hit on the head…?" Raphael let out an astonished voice, but eventually gave in, made a strained smile, and said, "Well, if the opportunity arises, I'll take you up on that offer."

"Well, I don't really get many chances to meet up with my friends from back home. It'd be, like, totally awkward to show my face after all this time!" Selphy explained her predicament, which was also the reason why she was glad Zagan was disregarding the conference.

"Raphael! Is that idiot Selphy around!?"

Selphy heard a somewhat familiar tone, but the voice was that of a child she didn't know. When she turned toward the source, she saw a young boy practically kicking down the door as he made his way into the kitchen. He seemed like an heir from some noble household, as he was wearing a dashing shirt and a stylish jacket. She felt like he resembled someone she knew, but Selphy wasn't acquainted with any children. It was entirely possible that he had been abducted by one of the sorcerers.

A kid? Did he get lost or something? Selphy stared at him in wonder, confused by the child's sudden appearance.

"Huh…? Sir… Zagan…?" Kimaris croaked out those words in a shocked voice.

"Oh, you're here too, Kimaris? Perfect. I was looking for you as well," the child answered in a somewhat haughty tone.

Why had Zagan's name popped out of Kimaris' mouth? Selphy assumed he must have been tired after all his work. It was either that or she'd heard wrong. She didn't know who brought this kid to the castle, but she pitied the fact that he was stuck here. And so, Selphy puffed out her chest as she stood before the boy.

"Hey now, you need to wash your hands when you enter the kitchen, you know? Mister Raphael will get angry if you don't. And you won't like his face when he's angry!"

"Shut it. More importantly, guide me to that conference or whatever it is. Right now."

"Man, you're one arrogant brat. Listen, you can't do that, okay? Only, like, Mister Raphael and Mister Zagan can be all haughty around here," Selphy said as she knit her brows.

"I'm telling you I'm Zagan!"

"Oh, okay. I guess that makes me, like, Miss Nephy. Mister Zagan spends a good twenty seconds tripping over his words when he talks to Miss Nephy, so you should— Owowowowowowowow!"

Selphy was an adult. She puffed her chest out proudly and decided to play house with the little kid, but her face was suddenly grasped by him like an eagle grabbing its prey.

"Why the hell do you know that!?"

"Owowowowowowowow!" Selphy screamed in agony. She didn't know why this kid was angry, but his strength was abnormal. And seeing that she would lose consciousness at this rate, Raphael cut in to stop him.

"My liege. If you keep that up, she'll die. Is that fine?"

"Oh... Sorry, I miscalculated my strength. Are you alright, Selphy?"

Luckily, the child let Selphy go before her head was actually crushed.

"Sir Zagan. What is with that form? Like I thought... did Miss Gremory do something again?" Kimaris inquired.

"No, she shares some of the blame, but it's not really her fault... Hey, are you alright? Should I have Nephy treat you?"

Since Selphy didn't seem to be recovering from the pain, the child peeked in at her face with worry.

He's pretty violent, but maybe he's not all that bad... Thinking that she couldn't make a kid worry about her, Selphy put on a smile and stood back up... Well, she had tears in her eyes, but that much could surely be forgiven.

"I'm okay! Your big sis here is a real tough cookie!"

"Hey, I'm telling you..."

As the child let out a troubled voice, Kimaris cut in to interrupt their display.

"Miss Selphy, this child is Sir Zagan. Even Miss Gremory is capable of turning into a child and an old woman, right?"

"Huh? You sure he isn't, like, Miss Gremory's grandkid or something?"

"..."

The entire group was dumbfounded by her stupidity. And so, they spent the next hour explaining that age manipulation sorcery existed, and that the boy before her was indeed Zagan.

"No way! Sorcery's, like, something that crazy!?"

"What did you even think it was before now?" Zagan stared straight at Selphy with an exasperated expression as he said that.

"I'm relying on you here, Selphy. Only you can help me return to my original form. Guide me to the conference," Zagan requested.

"But, like, I still find it hard to believe you're a small Zagan. Plus, it'd be totally awkward to show my face to my family, so I don't wanna," Selphy began grumbling and griping in response.

"You won't help me…?" Zagan slumped his shoulders, looking defeated.

"But, like, you were the one who saved me from that ship, and you even gave me a place to work. This time it's my turn to save you. Okay! I'll take you to that conference!" Selphy proclaimed as she proudly stuck out her chest.

"Really!? Thanks!" Zagan raised both his hands into the air to celebrate as he said that.

Now that I think about it, this is, like, the first time anyone's relied on me… Selphy was still scared of sorcery, but life in the castle was mostly comfortable, so she wanted to do whatever she could to protect that place of warmth.

"Alright! Since that's settled, let's get ready. I have to bring Nephy along this time, so we need to thoroughly prepare for the journey!" Zagan spoke those words in an overeager tone.

"Oh! Wait, can you, like, hold on a bit!?" Selphy called out to stop Zagan as he began dashing out of the kitchen.

"Is something wrong?"

"You're not gonna return to the castle for a while, right? In that case, I want you to listen to what Mister Raphael has to say."

"Stop, Selphy," Raphael raised his voice in a somewhat angry tone, but it was already too late.

"…What do you mean? Did something happen?" Zagan asked.

"No, it is not something that you need to worry about," Raphael responded in an obstinate manner. He had intended to keep it to himself, but Selphy had gone and ruined everything.

"Mister Raphael's been having some really weird dreams lately, so he wanted to, like, consult you about… Eeek!" Selphy babbled on about his issues, which made Raphael aim a death glare at her. Selphy curled into a ball in response, but Zagan turned about to face him anyway.

"Raphael. Speak."

"Urgh…" Raphael grimaced, but still found himself unable to deny Zagan's request. And so, he reluctantly told him all about his dreams.

"Orobas' memories?"

"Yes. It's likely about the last battle he fought by my side. However, what worries me is that he was fighting something that seemed different from a demon."

"What does that mean? Wasn't the demon you fought the one that's now a chimera in Archdemon Palace?"

"The one I butchered was that demon. However, that wasn't the only thing on that battlefield. It seems Orobas fought something far more powerful than a mere demon…"

"Impossible. The only one who could be that powerful is the Demon Lord. But…" Zagan held up his right hand, and a sigil of light glowed on surface as he continued, "The Demon Lord is sealed here. I've never heard of the thirteen sigils being broken."

At the very least, when Zagan first inherited the Sigil of the Archdemon, all thirteen were gathered together.

"That's why I also believe it to be impossible."

"…Then does that mean another major threat exists? No, that can't…" Zagan mumbled those words with his head hung low, then shook his head. If such powerful beings popped up that frequently, the world would have been destroyed long ago. However, it was also true that Wise Dragon Orobas, who lived through the age of myths, couldn't keep up with that enemy, so it had to have been extremely strong.

"Got it. I don't know the true nature of your dreams, but I'll keep them in mind. Was that your only worry?"

"No, there's something else you need to know," Raphael claimed as he shifted his focus over to Zagan's right hand before saying, "It seems Wise Dragon Orobas and Archdemon Marchosias were old friends. Also, it may have been a friendship that spanned a thousand years."

"...I just so happened to hear about that from Orias. This is the first I've heard of it spanning a thousand years, though," Zagan said as his eyes widened due to the sudden revelation. Thinking back on it, even though Zagan inherited Marchosias' legacy, he knew nothing about his predecessor. Sure, he had suddenly died of old age, but Zagan wished he had left a bit more information behind in preparation for his passing.

No, wait... Old age? I can't be... Zagan was taken aback.

"Raphael. When did you fight by Orobas' side? This is important, so think carefully."

"Hm... It's been about half a year now, so two months before I met you, my liege."

In other words, it would've been about one month before Zagan met Nephy. And from that, Kimaris definitely noticed what was on Zagan's mind.

"Oh... Sir Zagan, could that mean...?"

"...Yeah," Zagan replied as he clenched his teeth, seemingly astonished by his own ignorance.

"That's the exact same period of time Archdemon Marchosias passed away."

Am I an idiot? Why did I never suspect a thing?

"Then... are you saying Archdemon Marchosias also lost his life in that battle?" Raphael asked as his eyes widened due to the shock.

"It would be a reasonable assumption. Nephy only ended up at that auction where I bought her because he died so suddenly."

Originally, Nephy was set to be sold to Marchosias. It wasn't out of the realm of possibilities that he intended to use her to further extend his lifespan, but if that were the case, it was even more strange that she was still alive. If his remaining years were that short, it wouldn't have mattered whether demons or a Demon Lord was coming, he would have prioritized extending his own life. After all, most people would care about their own life above all else.

"Now that I think of it, I heard a conversation in my dream. I don't remember it very well, but I feel like Marchosias said something about sheltering someone," Raphael remarked, taken aback by it all.

"Sheltering? Not abducting, but sheltering? An Archdemon said that?"

"I do find it rather odd, but isn't it safe to assume he was talking about Lady Nephy?"

Why would an Archdemon want to shelter her? Sure, she's a high elf, but that isn't a good enough reason. Given her race, the idea that he planned on using her as a sacrifice seemed far more convincing...

Maybe I need to go over everything I know about Marchosias... They had likely learned all they could through discussing it between them, so it was time to move on. Plus, Zagan had to return his body to normal, which meant he had no time to waste.

"I understand. At any rate, I highly doubt those dreams are a mere coincidence. It may be some sort of warning. I'll keep my guard up as I travel, so don't let it cloud your judgment."

"As you wish," Raphael replied. Then, Zagan looked over to Selphy.

"As for you... Well, good work."

"Huh? Did I do something?"

"...It's nothing, really. I was just thinking it's good that we have someone as insensitive as you around."

"Ahahah, stop, you'll make me blush with those compliments!"

"Was that really a compliment?" Raphael asked as he looked over to Selphy. However, she paid his words no mind.

"Oh, right. While I'm being, like, all insensitive, can I say one more thing?"

"Are you self-aware that you're insensitive…? Well, fine. Owing to the occasion, speak your mind."

"Um, Miss Selphy, it would be better if you showed a bit more restraint," Kimaris said, completely on edge all the while, but Selphy simply puffed out her chest and ignored his warning.

"Mister Zagan, you should, like, rely on those around you more! That makes people, like, totally happy!"

"…Got it. I'll keep that in mind," Zagan blinked in surprise, then nodded with a strained smile as he said that.

"Ooooh… You know, when you're acting all honest and cute in this tiny form, my heart flutters! You should try talking like that to Miss Nephy, too!"

"…Do you want me to crush your face again?"

Zagan may have been tiny, but he was still the exact same person at heart. And so, Selphy turned white as a sheet as she vigorously shook her head.

"I see. You need a siren to guide you through the ocean," Zagan muttered those words to himself in admiration. It had been two days since he had decided to travel to the conference.

The ocean capital, Atlastia, was a metropolis at the bottom of the ocean far away from the continent where the Continental Interracial Elders Conference was being held. In fact, it was even far enough that a boat from Kianoides would have taken over a week to get there, but luckily, sirens could manipulate water currents. Using that power, it was possible to get there in a single day.

I only have four days until my date... In the end, Zagan never got a chance to buy new clothes. And at most, he had two free days to get ready. He had to hurry. That was why he looked at his surroundings in a panic. Since they were supposedly at the bottom of the ocean, there were countless fish swimming about above them. However, his field of vision was poor, so anything beyond ten paces appeared hazy. He was apparently at a depth where the light from the sun couldn't reach them, but mysteriously enough, it was bright as day around him. It was different from how sorcerers used sorcery to see in the dark. Having said that, it wasn't like there was a clear light source around. It was like the air... or rather, the water itself was shining.

It wasn't grass growing beneath his feet, but seaweed and coral. There wasn't any air around them at all, just ocean water. The reason he could breathe despite that seemed to be the power of the sirens.

This was apparently the entrance to a city or country, so he could spot something akin to a man-made temple in the distance. The stones sticking out around it seemed to have lights within them, and a closer inspection revealed windows and entrances. Though, for the time being, Zagan couldn't spot anybody present other than the fish.

"This is quite a mysterious place, isn't it?" Nephy asked in an entranced voice as her hand gripped Zagan's like a vice. Aside from her, only Foll, who also had to have the curse removed, and Selphy, who served as their guide, were accompanying Zagan. And since they were heading to the conference, Nephy was wearing a formal dress instead of her usual maid uniform.

Incidentally, Zagan and Foll had their usual clothes on for when they returned to their original forms. Though, it wasn't like they were wearing them underneath their current clothes or anything. Instead, they were using sorcery to fold space itself and have it cloaked around them, which almost made it seem like they were wearing invisible clothes.

Raphael and Kimaris stayed behind to watch the castle. *There's no way I can let my subordinates find out about this form, so they'd better keep them occupied...*

It wasn't like there were any among them that would start a revolt over such a thing, but being treated like a child was far too painful. Sure, they had no ill will, but it was still rather annoying.

"It's like being above the water and inside it at the same time. Feels weird," Foll said as she gave him a small nod. They were walking around normally, and it didn't feel like their clothes were wet at all. Or so they thought, but Selphy was swimming about in the air. In a way, it was like they were walking through a thick, lingering fog, which probably meant there was a barrier set up in the area. However, if there was, it was terrifyingly enormous.

"It's not sorcery, but it's also different from a dragon's power… If I had to compare it to something, elven mysticism seems like the best fit."

Is this one of the lost powers that reside in Liucaon? This conference was closer to Liucaon than the continent. It was said that a power different from sorcery remained in that island nation, which filled Zagan with hope.

"It does feel similar, doesn't it? I sense something like the power of spirits that shouldn't be in the water here. Perhaps they're borrowing power from such beings?" Nephy muttered while observing her surroundings.

"Seems it's, like, the power of some Holy Treasure that's been passed down through the royal family," Selphy replied in a rather indifferent tone.

"…Is it fine for you to reveal that to outsiders?"

"Huh, aren't we all, like, family?"

"I've heard that servants are just like family, so you are," Foll nodded her head and gave that reply in Zagan's place as he was too embarrassed to answer Selphy.

"Wow! You're saying we're, like, really close, right!?" Selphy exclaimed, clearly seeming quite happy. Zagan didn't understand why she would ever be pleased by Foll's statement, but he didn't bother mentioning it.

"Anyway, this is my kingdom. Though, there's only, like, a few hundred people living here, so it's totally more of a small village."

Like the elves and dragons, sirens were an endangered species. And since only several hundred residents lived in this kingdom, it was hard to imagine them surviving the next hundred years. Luckily, its existence was a closely guarded secret. If sorcerers ever managed to sniff it out, sirens would go extinct overnight.

"Is that conference or whatever always held here?"

"Dunno. But, like, this is the first time I've seen it myself, so they probably move it around, right?"

"I'm surprised you can call yourself royalty when you know so little."

"Haha... I mean, isn't it, like, hard to remember things you aren't interested in?"

"Now that I think of it, what races are coming?" Nephy turned to Selphy and asked her that question. However, Selphy simply cocked her head to the side as if she'd never even given the matter any thought, which made total sense.

"Let's see. I don't know how many races gather for this conference, but the rarer ones are dragons like Foll, as well as elves like Nephy or Nephteros," Zagan cut in to answer Nephy's question. Then, he stuck out his fingers as he began counting them down by saying, "Other than that, there are fomorians like Gremory, leonins like Kimaris, tabaxi like Kuroka... Oh, and I've heard there are fairies too. Though, the term fairies encompasses a lot. Elves and cait sith are included in that category."

"Are tabaxi and cait sith different races?" Nephy tilted her head to the side as she asked that question.

"For the time being. Having said that, it's only a matter of whether their human or cat portions are more prominent, so they're largely considered the same. However, the quality of their mana is clearly different, so sorcerers definitely note the difference."

"Yup! Also, I've heard that cait siths possess a similar amount of mana to sirens and succubi! The three of them are, like, quite special in Liucaon!" Selphy exclaimed as she thrust her right hand into the air.

"I see. You're quite knowledgeable, aren't you?" Nephy replied.

"Hehehe. I'm a siren, too. Those old geezers would totally have, like, yelled at me if I didn't learn this much," Selphy explained. Unfortunately, it likely took all the effort said geezers could muster to force just that little information into her head.

"Those are all of the rarer species. Avians like Manuela, lycans, canuses, and dwarves can be found anywhere you look. Other than that..." Zagan trailed off as he thought of other races. Then, a certain name suddenly came to mind, so he said, Hm... I don't know if they'd be included among the continent's races, but... the Night Clan. There are a lot who go by that name."

It was likely Nephy's first time hearing that name, as her ears quivered, which showed her interest in the matter.

"What are they like?"

"To put it simply, they're undead. However, they're fundamentally different from the zombies and skeletons sorcerers create. They can survive without being supplied mana, and they can't be killed. Though, you can apparently break them into small enough pieces to stop them from taking any kind of action," Zagan replied. He was unsure if even Heaven's Phosphor was powerful enough to finish them off, since their constitution was rather unique. Having said that, Zagan had never met one.

"Wow, there's someone that scary here, huh!? I wonder if they'll listen to me sing?" Selphy let out a thoughtless laugh as she said that, seemingly not noticing Nephy turn pale next to her.

"Who knows? Well, the church has their eyes on them, so you'll never see them on the continent. Anyway, they're strong, which about sums them up."

From the way Selphy was speaking, it seemed the Night Clan had nothing to do with the conference.

And, as they were talking about such things, they arrived at the temple. It was an old building made of a strange material that was neither metal nor stone. He didn't know what wear and tear was like under the sea, but still, based on the thick seaweed and sediment stuck to it, he guessed it had been around for at least two hundred years. There were several lights set up around it, and it seemed like something was there, but...

"Zagan. Someone's coming," Foll raised her voice in alarm while Zagan was taking in his new surroundings. Then, she pointed at a girl who was running toward them, yelling something and waving about her hand with all her might.

"Oh! Isn't that Lilith!? Heeey, Lilith! It's me! The siren, Selphooomph!?" Selphy shouted out in joy upon seeing her and swam toward the girl, but she was cut off by a merciless slap.

"You big dummy! Why are you acting so casual about all this!? No princess from of one of the three great royal families has ever run away from home, you know!? Don't you realize you're in for a huge scolding!? And hey, how come you didn't even try contacting me at all!?"

Her final sentence seemed unconnected to all the rest, but it had made it apparent that she was Selphy's friend. Selphy was drifting in the air with her eyes spinning about, but soon enough, she regained her consciousness and started laughing without an ounce of timidness in her voice.

"Ahahah, sorry about that. But listen, if I got in touch, those old geezers would've totally found me. I'm, like, really sorry, so don't cry, Lilith."

"I-I'm not crying you dummy! What you're doing out there has nothing to do with me!"

Before they knew it, the girl who slapped Selphy hugged her with tears in her eyes. Apparently, in contrast to her sharp tongue, she was a good person on the inside.

"...Gremory would jump for joy if she saw this," Zagan stated in a monotonous voice.

"...You're right. Not bringing her was a good choice," Foll readily agreed.

And with that, the girl looked over to Zagan's group, having finally noticed them.

She looked to be about the same age as Selphy, at 15 or 16 years old. Her vivid crimson hair was tied up at both sides of her face, and she had horns growing out of her head. She looked almost like Gremory, but the bat-like wings on her back were a rather obvious difference.

A succubus, huh? They were a race who could apparently traverse the world of dreams. This was Zagan's first time meeting one, and she appeared to be someone of high standing, since she was wearing a frilly one-piece dress and had a nice necktie draped over her back.

"And who are you? Some spoiled little brat?" Lilith wiped away her tears, then aimed a glare at Zagan as she asked that question.

Well, I guess this is Selphy's home... It wasn't all that unusual to find others like her around the area.

"Oh, this is my lord, Mister Zagan. And, the ones behind him are, like, his… wife? Fiancee? Well, that's Miss Nephy and their daughter, Foll. Guys, this girl is my childhood friend, Lilith."

"Um, daughter…? What's that supposed to mean? And how does he have a fiancee at his age? Is he someone important?"

"It'll take, like, way too long to explain! I'll tell you all about it later."

"When have you ever said that and properly explained things?"

Ugh, this is so annoying. I just want to ask around about the curse and get out of here… Perhaps having noticed Zagan's irritation, Nephy let go of his hand and faced Lilith.

"It's a pleasure to meet you. I am Nephelia, Master Zagan's disciple, maid… and recently, I've become his lover."

"Hm…? Wait, hold on… I feel like… I've heard the name Zagan before…?" Lilith cocked her head to the side in confusion as she said that.

"Why don't you introduce yourself as well?" Nephy asked with a flat smile on her face. Her voice had a somewhat cold ring to it, which made the succubus involuntarily gulp.

"Uh, right… My name, huh? Very well. Clean out your ears and listen carefully. I am Lilithiera Fauna Hypnoel, first princess of the succubi and descendant of the proud Silver-Eyed King. I am a member of the three great royal families, so do remember to pay your respect!"

"Is that so? Well, Miss Lilithiera, though it is rather presumptuous of me to say this, allow me to give you a single piece of advice," Nephy said that as she clasped the girl's shoulder with a thud, then put on a refreshing smile and continued, "I am not so gentle that I will continue to just smile when someone is ridiculing my lord."

The atmosphere froze over instantly.

Crap, this is bad. Nephy's mad... She was a girl who never let her anger show on the surface, but it seemed she was overly sensitive due to Zagan's transformation.

"Sh-Sh-Sh-Shorry..." Lilith stumbled over her apology as she began trembling and tears welled up in her eyes. She was scared enough to faint at any moment, so even Zagan sympathized with her.

"It's fine, Nephy. Don't get so mad. A brat should be disciplined by their parents, right?" Zagan requested she just leave it at that, and Nephy obliged with a dissatisfied expression on her face. After being freed from that pressure, Lilith weakly sank to her knees.

"Nephy, you got too mad. Bad children should be scolded, not hurt," Foll claimed as she turned to Nephy with a look of pity for Lilith in her eyes.

"Oh... You're... right. My apologies, Miss Lilithiera, I went too far," Nephy bowed as she said that, having finally returned to her senses.

"You okay?" Foll asked as she held her hand out to Lilith.

"H-Hmph! This is nothing... Wait, what!?" Lilith let out a scream.

"What's wrong?"

"Wh-What's wrong? Wh-What... What are you? Why does something like this exist in the world...?"

Hm? Has she noticed that Foll's a dragon? The succubi were a rare species, but they had little in the way of actual strength, especially when compared to dragons. That was why her reaction was perfectly...

"Ohhh, Lilith, your tits still haven't, like, grown at all, huh?" Selphy unleashed that cruel statement in a casual manner, which made Lilith pin down her flat chest bitterly. She had been hit with those words right after being scolded by Nephy, which just made the whole thing too much for a girl in her teens. Lilith fell to her knees once more, going silent as her face twisted due to the humiliation of it all.

"Why did you get so mad? Usually, you would try to teach a bad child to act better," Foll turned to Nephy and asked her that question due to the immense feeling of pity that was welling up within her.

"That's… Master Zagan suffered through a harsh childhood, just like I did, but unlike me, he's working hard to move past it. That's why I took it as a personal insult, since that would make me even worse…"

"I see. That's what set you off, huh?" Zagan said, ruffling his hair as he came to an understanding. Unlike what she claimed, her reaction seemed to give away the fact that she was angry about someone she loved being insulted in front of her.

Perhaps Nephy's memories have taken on a new meaning… Her change in expression and displays of emotion were things he believed she carried back from the hidden elven village. Initially, he assumed it had only happened because she had been turned into a child, but maybe visiting her old home triggered a change instead…

"Hear me, Nephy. The truly strong are not affected by such trivial heckling. Do not lower yourself to her level," Zagan ordered.

"Master Zagan…" Nephy mumbled as she crouched before Zagan, then replied in a dignified voice, "People are constantly wounded by thoughtless words. Not feeling anything when faced with them is a sign that your heart has frozen over. That's why it's best to get angry when you're insulted."

Zagan couldn't believe he had forgotten something that simple. And so, he shot a glare over at Lilith, since he blamed her for Nephy scolding him.

"I see… You really are the one at fault here!"

"What's with this brat!?" Lilith roared out those words as tears ran down her cheeks, leaving Foll and Selphy dumbfounded.

"That's so petty, Zagan…"

"This is, like, the first time I've seen Mister Zagan be such a big, fat jerk…"

Well, it's true that I wouldn't normally make such a lame excuse in front of Nephy… Zagan thought as he groaned in the face of their reproachful stares. However, luckily, Nephy had a pleasant smile on her face, which cheered him right up.

"Master Zagan is cute when he's childish," Nephy claimed. His reaction seemed to satisfy her. And upon seeing her rare happy expression, he felt himself go weak in the knees. However, Foll seemed to have her own thoughts on the matter.

"This Zagan is different from when he's an adult? Isn't the only difference between a child and adult their power?" Foll, whose body only grew bigger, asked, as she was seemingly unable to understand the differences between adults and children. Feeling sorry for her, Zagan stretched his hand out to Foll's head.

"…Zagan, what are you doing?"

He was stretching out his hand to pat his daughter's head, but he couldn't get anywhere close to it in his current form.

"I can't reach. Lower your head."

"Like this?" Foll asked as she lowered down with reservation, which finally let Zagan brush her head.

"Hear me, Foll. People accumulate intelligence as they grow up. And I believe intelligence is not just knowledge, but the ability to understand."

"The ability to understand...?"

"That's right. Listen, Foll, you may have attained the body of an adult, but you've yet to accumulate such intelligence. You'll never learn the true difference between an adult and a child unless you look past the surface level."

"That's hard to understand," Foll claimed as she folded her arms and puzzled over the idea for a while.

"I may look young now, but I'm still your parent. I'll be strict with you when I have to."

"Are you saying Lilith is still a child?" Foll asked as she shifted her gaze over to Lilith.

"...It's good to see that you at least understand that much."

"Hey, you lot! Don't think you'll get off lightly after making a fool of the next head of the succubi! I'll put in a formal complaint to the church!" Lilith roared as she turned bright red due to Zagan and Foll's comments. However, upon hearing the word church, everyone aside from her cocked their heads to the side.

"What does the church have to do with anything?"

"What? I mean, you people... don't seem to be from the church... Huh? Wait, who are you?" Lilith inquired. It seemed she had misread them entirely up to that point.

"Huh? Lilith, didn't you, like, come to greet us?"

"I didn't. This is your home, so there's no need for me to guide you, right? I came here to—" Lilith cut herself off as she felt someone approaching them.

"Hello there. Is this the location of the Continental Interracial Elders Conference?"

It was none other than Archangel Chastille Lillqvist.

Why is Chastille here? Zagan's body stiffened upon hearing that familiar voice. And upon looking behind her, he noticed that Nephteros and Kuroka were accompanying her. There were several other Angelic Knights as well, but perhaps out of good fortune, the three idiots weren't among them.

As he wondered why she was there, Zagan recalled Raphael's words from earlier. *"The representative for the humans is selected from the church, after all."*

He had mentioned that Chastille would be their most likely choice, but Zagan hadn't really been expecting to see her. And so, he hid behind Nephy in a fluster.

"Nephy? Wait, why are you here?" Chastille asked as her eyes widened in surprise.

"Chastille? Um, well, that's rather hard to answer..." Nephy trailed off as she tried to think up an excuse. Zagan had wanted his situation to be kept secret, but she wasn't very good at lying, so she just looked troubled as she spoke with her head cocked to the side.

"Hm...? Hold on... Uh, I don't think it's possible, but is the one over there... Foll?" Chastille asked, clearly confused as she looked over to Foll.

"Yeah. It's me. You got it despite not being a sorcerer. How admirable, Horse Head," Foll replied.

"What happened? Also, is it just you two? I don't see Zagan anywhere... Does he know you two are here?" Chastille inquired as she began to massage her brow as if she was getting a headache.

"That's, um…"

Crap. Chastille's in her work mode… She was usually a huge crybaby, and a total wreck, but that all changed when she was on duty. That made her extremely reliable as an ally, but that wasn't what Zagan needed at the moment.

"What are you saying, Lady Chastille? Isn't he standing right there?" Kuroka said as she pointed straight at Zagan, her triangular ears twitching curiously.

"Huh?"

Right. She distinguishes people by their scent and presence, doesn't she? Zagan may have shrunk, but nothing else about him had really changed. And so, it seemed Kuroka's perception of Zagan hadn't been altered either.

"Wait a minute… What's going on?" Nephteros asked, seemingly bewildered.

"H-Hold on… Who is that kid? Why does he look so much like Zagan? Don't tell me…!" Chastille's eyes shot open as if she'd just realized the truth before she continued, "Is he Nephy and Zagan's illegitimate child!?"

I see she's back to her usual self now… It seemed that despite being in work mode, the shock of it all had made her revert to her normal state. Sensing that continuing to keep quiet would only cause further problems, Zagan reluctantly stepped forward.

"You reacted the exact same way when you first saw Foll."

"Huh!? If you know that, then… No way, are you really Zagan?"

"If you want to laugh, then go right ahead. I ended up like this after failing some sorcery."

"…I won't laugh. How did a sorcerer of your level end up like this?" Chastille asked that question, hoping to hear a response, but…

"HAHAHAHAHAHA! You serious? You're really Zagan!?"

Damn it. How'd I forget? If Chastille is here, then so's that idiot... Zagan facepalmed as a gloomy man suddenly crept out of the shadow at Chastille's feet. It was Barbatos.

"HAHAHAHAHAHA! I can't believe it! This dumb kid is Zagan? Guess it's time to get some payback. I'll finish you off and become an ArchdAMPH!"

Zagan's fist sank right into Barbatos' cheek before he finished speaking. He instantly broke through his molars, then drove him down to the stone floor of the sea. Eventually, the bedrock caved in, and Barbatos' face vanished into it.

Chastille put her hand to her head, looking almost embarrassed, while Kuroka seemed to be deeply moved, since she was clapping her hands. Foll and Nephteros, on the other hand, didn't seem to care at all, while Nephy formed a strained smile as if it was a common sight. The clear outliers were Selphy and Lilith, who were trembling as they hugged each other.

"Hm... I meant to kill him with that, but it seems this form is limiting me," Zagan claimed as he looked down at the hand he used to strike Barbatos. The number of circuits he could construct at once hadn't been reduced, but it seemed there was now a limit to how much he could increase his strength. He was unable to bring out even twenty percent of his full power.

This is a huge problem... He had to fix it before they got into any trouble. By that point, Kuroka also seemed to have noticed something was amiss, so she stepped forward while knitting her brows.

"Um... Mister, are you... crouching?" Kuroka asked, likely judging Zagan's height based on where his voice was coming from. However, it seemed she hadn't discerned that he turned into a child yet.

Well, the cat's already out of the bag, so I shouldn't leave her out... Zagan took Kuroka's hand and placed it against his own face. He had heard before that the blind could grasp the shape of people's faces by touching them.

"U-Um... No, wait, huh?" Kuroka's eyes shot open in astonishment as she began trembling.

"Do you get it now? This is my current form," Zagan stated.

"Oh... I see..." Kuroka replied. It seemed she may have hated touching people's faces, since her hand was still shaking.

"Oops, my bad," Zagan said as he released her hand. And once he did, she shrank back extremely fast.

"Kuroka, what's wrong?" Nephteros asked as she shifted over to her companion.

"Oh, it's just... my hands... are dirty... so touching someone's face is a little..." Kuroka trailed off, but it was obvious that she was feeling rather embarrassed. It seemed Nephteros and Kuroka had grown quite close while living at the church, which pleased Zagan immensely.

"Huh... Kuroka? Just now... you said Kuroka, right?" Lilith asked as she gulped audibly.

"Hm? They don't look dirty to me. Did you touch something filthy recently?" Nephteros knit her brows and asked that question without paying Lilith any mind at all.

"Um, uh, yes! I don't really know what it was, but it felt squishy!"

"Seriously...? Hey, siren, are you a local? Is there some place she can wash her hands?"

However, before Selphy could answer, Lilith raised her desperate voice.

"Hey! Are you... Kuroka? The one from house Adelhide!?"

"Huh...? Yes. That's me," Kuroka nodded despite her confusion.

"It's me! The succubus Lilithiera! You played with me and Selphy a lot, right!?" Lilith exclaimed as tears began to well up in her eyes.

"You're... Lilith?" Kuroka muttered as her eyes widened in surprise. And upon hearing that, Lilith threw her arms around Kuroka.

"WAAAAAAAAAH! I was so worried! You could have at least let us know you were still alive, you big dummy!"

"Sorry. Um... a lot of things happened."

They know each other... Kuroka was a therianthrope from Liucaon, Lilith was royalty there, and Selphy was a resident of the ocean that tied it to the continent. It wasn't all that strange that they were connected in some way. Plus, they were all close in age, so it made sense that they were childhood friends.

"Wow! What a coincidence! Kuroka, can you, like, tell who I am?" Selphy asked as she joined in on their hug.

"You're the same as ever, I see. I remember you," Kuroka replied. She was being jostled around by the unruly pair, but looked considerably happy regardless.

"So, like, how are Aunty and Uncle doing?" Selphy asked. Unfortunately, it seemed she had not managed to read the air.

"I see. Now that I think of it, you ran away from home before it happened..." Lilith muttered as her face stiffened.

"Huh? What do you mean?" Selphy asked as she cocked her head to the side. However, it seemed a little cruel to make Kuroka explain it herself, so Zagan stepped forward.

"Kuroka's people have perished. She's currently being sheltered by the church. Right, Chastille?"

It was about time for Chastille to recover from her shock. And as he shifted the focus over to her, Chastille returned an firm nod.

"Yeah. Pastor Kuroka is doing splendid work at the church, and is currently serving as my advisor. She's been a big help."

"Then, is that also why your eyes…?" Selphy's sense of endless optimism seemed to fade as she asked that question.

"Yes. Like I said… a lot has happened…" Kuroka replied with a troubled smile, which made Selphy droop her shoulders and hang her head.

"I didn't know at all… Sorry…"

"You've got no reason to apologize. Besides, someone saved me, so I've got no regrets," Kuroka claimed as she looked toward Zagan.

"I don't know what you mean. Honestly, you should be thanking Raphael. It had nothing to do with me," Zagan replied as he shrugged his shoulders.

"I see… Even you get embarrassed, huh, Mister?"

Kuroka said before slapping Lilith on the back and asking, "Come on, aren't you here because of your duties?"

"…I-I-I know that."

Having finally remembered why she was there, Lilith turned bright red and took her distance. And even though her eyes were still red and swollen, the succubus lifted the hems of her frilly skirt and curtsied before them.

"I apologize for my late introduction. My name is Lilithiera Fauna Hypnoel. I've been sent to guide the representatives from the church. Would it be correct to assume that you are the envoys?"

It seemed Lilith had been sent to serve as the guide for Chastille's group. Her declaration made the entire church group stand to attention.

"Archangel Chastille Lillqvist. It seems that Pastor Kuroka requires no introduction, but this is my personal friend, Nephteros. And the others are my subordinates. We'll be in your care."

"...And who's that?" Lilith asked as she pointed at Barbatos, who was still buried headfirst in the ground.

"An ally... probably?" Chastille replied hesitantly. She probably still disliked the idea of calling such a heinous sorcerer a friend, which was only natural, but...

Did something happen? Zagan felt something other than simple disgust in Chastille's words. And while he stood around, trying to piece things together, Chastille walked over to Lilith.

"He'll join us eventually, so just leave him be for now."

"Is that so...? Well, whatever. The ocean capital is protected by the sirens' Holy Treasure, so an ordinary sorcerer is no real threat."

Selphy had mentioned it before, but it seemed there really was a Holy Treasure here. And it was a weapon on par with the Sacred Swords.

"Speaking of Holy Treasures, is it similar to the one enshrined in Liucaon? I'm interested in it as a wielder of a Sacred Sword."

"That's just a replica, so I doubt it has much power. As for the original..." Lilith glanced over to Kuroka. And perhaps noticing her gaze, Kuroka returned a nod.

"Liucaon's Holy Treasure is known as the Moonless Sky. It consists of a pair of opposing swords."

"Huh, a pair of swords? You can't mean..." Chastille's face stiffened as her words trailed off.

"Yes. My people were the ones who enshrined the Moonless Sky," Kuroka stated as she drew her blades. That really surprised Zagan and Nephteros.

Is that why those shortswords reacted to celestial mysticism? If that were the case, the Holy Treasures were likely related to the Sacred Swords and the elves.

143

"Selphy's house Neptuna, Kuroka's house Adelhide, and my house Hypnoel are the three great royal families who've inherited the Holy Treasures of Liucaon," Lilith stated as she proudly puffed out her chest.

In other words, there are only three Holy Treasures... Kuroka's shortswords were as strong as a Sacred Sword. The idea that a small island nation like Liucaon had three such artifacts in their possession was quite terrifying. Still, that meant there was a possibility that one of them could cure him.

"Now then, dear guests. We don't know if the last invitees are even coming, so you're probably the last ones," Lilith said as she pointed toward the temple.

"My apologies for being late... Wait, who's missing?"

"The new Archdemon. He never sent a reply, so he probably won't be coming."

"Huh? By Archdemon, you mean..." Chastille looked over to Zagan, but he held his finger to his lips to urge her to stay silent.

I don't give a damn about this conference. I'm just here to find a way to regain my true form... He really didn't have time to speak to strangers.

"You're tagging along, aren't you, Kuroka? Do you have time to talk?"

"Yes. Let's catch up, Lilith."

Selphy said nothing as she watched her two childhood friends walk away. And after a short while, Zagan roughly slapped her back.

"That hurt, Mister Zagan..."

"Like I care. Listen, you're too noisy, so you make us stand out. Get lost."

"By that, you mean, I should... like, go with Lilith and the others?" Selphy asked as she stared back at Zagan in surprise.

"...I don't care where you go. Do whatever you want."

"Thanks. I'll, like, totally never forget this debt, or what you did for Kuroka!" Selphy patted Zagan's head with sparkles in her eyes as she said that.

"Whatever. Just get going already, you damn nuisance."

After Zagan cruelly thrust her away, Selphy waved her arm about in the air so vigorously that it felt like it would tear off at any moment before running after her friends.

"Why must they always exaggerate," Zagan said as he let out a snort.

"I don't believe that's the case," Nephy refuted before continuing, "Even if you claim it was no big deal, you saved all those girls. That's why I believe you should honestly accept their gratitude."

"Hm..."

For whatever reason, Nephy seemed a lot more strict when Zagan was in this form. Or wait, was kind a more fitting word? Either way, her reactions were quite different from usual, which troubled Zagan.

Gratitude huh? He didn't really care about receiving gratitude, but he knew he was very bad at expressing it. Honestly, he had barely ever done it.

This is bad... Zagan thought as he cleared out his throat with a cough.

"Then, Nephy..." Zagan stretched out his hand, but he couldn't reach Nephy's head in his current form. However, he managed to touch Nephy's bangs when he stood on his toes. And as he did, Nephy sensed what he was trying to do and lightly lowered her head.

"Is this fine?"

"Y-Yes," Zagan said as he began awkwardly brushing Nephy's head.

"Nephy, thanks for getting angry on my behalf earlier. Still, there's no need to force yourself. I prefer... the usual you."

Was Zagan able to properly convey his feelings? It wasn't hard to tell, since the tips of Nephy's ears turned bright red.

"That's not fair, Master Zagan. Saying such things at a time like this is..." Nephy trailed off, then placed her own hand atop Zagan's hand. She didn't say anything more, but she didn't let his hand go, either. They simply remained like that for a while before Foll interrupted them.

"Zagan, Nephteros is coming back."

"What!?" Zagan and Nephy exclaimed as they separated from each other in a fluster. Perhaps due to good fortune, visibility was poor, so Nephteros didn't seem to really suspect anything as she walked up to Zagan's group. There was a young Angelic Knight following her, but his face didn't look familiar.

"Please wait, Lady Nephteros. It's dangerous for you to walk about on your own."

"Shouldn't you be escorting Chastille? There's no need to follow me."

"You are also someone I've sworn to protect. I shall remain by your side."

It seemed that he was there to keep an eye on Nephteros, or guard her, or whatever.

His strength... is somewhere near the top, huh? He was at least an equal match for the three idiots. However, he was nowhere close to Chastille or Kuroka.

"What's wrong? Shouldn't you be with Chastille?"

"Um, Kuroka and the others are there, so they should be fine. More importantly…" Nephteros trailed off and averted her gaze. The tips of her pointy ears then quivered as she gathered her resolve and said, "You're troubled by this turn of events, right? I'll lend you a hand."

Even her dark skin turned bright red as she said that.

I see… She's probably been practicing those lines this entire time, huh? Zagan was charmed by that and squinted his eyes. If his sister-in-law was trying this hard, there was no point turning her down. And so, he decided to accept her offer.

"Sure. Thanks. I'm not even sure what I need right now, but I'll be relying on you."

"Th-That's a little hard to handle. You shouldn't pressure me like that!" Nephteros turned her face away in a huff, though Zagan didn't overlook the faint smile that rose to her face.

"You're so cute, Nephteros!" Foll exclaimed.

"Huh…? Wait, you're… Foll, right? Does you becoming bigger have something to do with this?"

"Yeah. But before that… welcome back, Nephteros," Foll said as she hugged her tightly.

Foll was really worried about Nephteros…

"…I'm back," Nephteros replied in an earnest tone. And after that, her gaze naturally shifted to Nephy.

"…"

A heavy silence fell over them.

This is bad… In truth, this was their first real meeting since the incident atop Bifrons' ship. They had meet at the hidden elven village, but Nephteros wasn't exactly in a calm state of mind back then, so they only exchanged a few short, polite words. And by the time night came, Nephy had been turned into a child.

147

Plus, although Zagan had mentioned who was sheltering her, he had never informed Nephy that he had accepted her as a sister-in-law, which was tied directly to her growth. That was why he continued to nervously watch over the two elves. And, as he worried about what to do, one of them spoke up.

"It has been quite a while, Miss Nephteros. I've heard that you are currently staying with Chastille. Do you find it to be inconvenient in any way?"

"...Not really. That girl is irritatingly attentive, and the people of the church are also very kind."

"That's a relief. Still, please let me know if you're ever troubled by anything. I'll do whatever I can to help."

Nephy's trying to probe their distance... Zagan was completely astonished by that fact. If she acted overly familiar, Nephteros would reject. But having said that, if she acted too reserved and treated her coldly, the distance between them would only increase. Despite the fine line, Nephy was somehow managing to walk that tightrope.

"Do you not... resent me at all?" Nephteros asked as she hung her head.

"Huh? Why would I?" Nephy asked as she stood there with a confused look on her face.

"Why? I mean, I deserve your scorn, don't I? Um, I attacked you, and pretended to be you... There's... a lot I've done..."

I see. Nephteros must feel extremely guilty... I hadn't expected that. It made sense that she regretted her actions, but Zagan had just assumed she would try to justify her actions instead of accepting all the blame.

It seems Chastille really did save this girl... Zagan honestly admired her change in character.

"There's no way I can just stay angry forever," Nephy replied with a somewhat bitter smile on her face. And those words seemed to set Nephteros off, as her expression shifted to one of indignation.

"What's with that? Quit trying to act like the bigger person!"

"No, that's not what I'm doing..." Nephy muttered. And, in an usual turn, she folded her arms together and began thinking before eventually replying, "You didn't do anything like crush a little songbird that's been my friend for years before my very eyes, or ignore me for a full sixteen years despite living in the same house, or say, 'You shouldn't even be allowed to live,' right? Well, that means you haven't done enough to make me truly hate you."

Nephy formed a bitter smile again after saying all that.

"Personally, those are the kind of memories I consider painful. I hated the things you did, Miss Nephteros, but they weren't bad enough to make me hold a grudge..."

"Haven't you... had a much harder life than me?" Nephteros inquired as she began to find it difficult to speak.

"I wonder? In my opinion, painful memories differ between people. For example, Master Zagan has gone through much more painful ordeals than I have, but he treats them like they're no big deal."

"No, really, my case wasn't all that serious. It's just stuff like my first memory being that of a rat-infested sewer I called home, or the times I got beaten to the verge of death for trying to steal food or money. Honestly, I had it pretty good," Zagan answered, panicking as the conversation turned to him. There was the young man who shared his bread with him, the young girl who read him a picture book, and so many other people he loosely considered friends, which meant he had not truly suffered.

In his mind, true suffering was loneliness. Loneliness was an unbearable pain to those who once knew the warmth of others, but also a poisonous worm that ate away at human emotions if they didn't. Or well, that was how it affected Zagan, at any rate. No matter what he did, he couldn't find any meaning in life, and he felt absolutely nothing. However, he disliked the idea of dying miserably more than anything else, so he simply continued to accumulate power.

"You guys had it hard..." Foll said with a light groan.

"This is the first time I've realized my own powerlessness since joining the Angelic Knights..." Richard, the young Angelic Knight who had remained silent so far, started to tear up. And perhaps because his grief was infectious, Nephteros also let out a depressing sigh.

"...It would be foolish to even try to compete," Nephteros mumbled as she brushed back her hair and continued, "I will continue to call you Nephelia. I know I've been told you're my elder sister, but it's hard to accept that right away."

"Yes. I do not min— Huh? Elder sister...?" Nephy's pointy ears stiffened as she lost her train of thought. Then, she aimed her bewildered gaze at Zagan.

"Oh... Um, well, that's just how it is. Nephteros is actually your little sister, so... I've decided to accept her as my sister-in-law."

"Huh? You didn't tell her?" Nephteros seemed to doubt her ears, which made Zagan avert his gaze.

I can't tell her I forgot because my mind got so caught up on planning our date... Naturally, there was also the fact that he couldn't mention Nephteros' upbringing, but still, he could have at least mentioned it indirectly.

"P-Please wait a moment. There were no other white-haired elves in that village. And if there were, they would have suffered much like I did, so a little sister would be…" Nephy remarked in a bewildered tone.

"O-Oh. That's also something I meant to tell you. You see, Nephteros wasn't born in that village, and neither were you. You were just entrusted to them because your mother was worried about you being targeted if you remained among other high elves."

Nephy stumbled around upon hearing that stunning revelation.

"Nephelia!" Nephteros cried as she moved to support her. Unfortunately, Zagan's childish arms were far too short to reach her.

Why won't my body listen to me! Zagan bit down on his lip in frustration at his powerlessness.

"…Come on. Keep it together. This should be no sweat. You just said nothing I did even fazed you, remember?" Nephteros spoke in a blunt tone. Her words sounded almost scornful, but Zagan could tell that was just her way of encouraging people. Nephy surely understood that as well, since before long, she stood up on her own two feet.

"My apologies. I was just… a little surprised," Nephy claimed before gripping Nephteros' hand and saying, "I was… never truly alone. This feeling is probably… happiness… I think?"

"I-I see," Nephteros replied as her ears quivered.

"Then, Miss Nephteros, do you know anything about our mother?"

"Um, I've only met her once, so not really… Still, she's alive."

"Is that so…" Nephy's tone made it clear that she felt both relieved and hurt at the same time.

"Are you happy? Or do you resent her?"

"I wonder…? This is all too sudden, so I'm not quite sure how I feel…"

"…Well, that's understandable."

Even Nephteros was still in the middle of putting her feelings in order, so Nephy's confusion made total sense.

"Anyway, stop calling me Miss Nephteros. I've been using just your first name this whole time."

"You have, haven't you? Understood… Nephteros."

This indescribably awkward moment was when the two of them finally recognized each other as sisters.

Zagan went over their predicament again once Nephteros joined up with them.

"So you're here to find something other than sorcery that can fix your issue?"

"I'm ashamed to admit it, but yes."

"Even Archdemon Orias threw in the towel, so there's really nothing for you to be ashamed of," Nephteros commented, then folded her arms and said, "I understand the situation, but in that case, wouldn't it be better to actually attend the conference? Surely the elders would be your best bet."

"Why would I go there when they're debating the fate of strangers? I don't care about any of that, and if I go to ask them for help, they'll attach troublesome conditions."

"Yeah, you definitely don't care at all…" Nephteros said as she rolled her eyes.

"What are you trying to say?" Zagan asked.

"Well, it's a little hard to believe that when you helped Kuroka and I after speaking to us only once or twice," Nephteros replied. And in response, Zagan simply cocked his head to the side as he mulled over his actions.

"It's certainly true that if Master Zagan met them, he would try to shoulder all their burdens himself. We should wait for the conference to end before doing anything," Nephy said with an air of delight in her voice.

Even Nephy's saying that? Hearing his bride reiterate Nephteros' point made Zagan squat down and cover his face. He was shocked that he had failed at playing the part of an arrogant Archdemon.

"In that case, can't we just go kidnap someone?" Barbatos inquired.

"That's a viable option, but this is their domain. As I am now, that would be a dangerous choice, so it should be our last resort," Zagan responded. They possessed treasures that were on par with Sacred Swords and had power that was neither sorcery nor mysticism, which made them a very real threat.

"Wait, really? Tch… You're right. My shadows won't open properly."

Everyone present cocked their heads upon hearing that. And, after turning around, they finally noticed that Barbatos had recovered and joined in on their conversation.

"When the hell did you wake up?"

"Huh? Somewhere around 'I prefer the usual you,' I think?"

"Wait, Zagan. The handyman's pretty handy. It'd be a waste to kill him now," Foll said as she quickly scooped Zagan up and stopped him before he finished Barbatos off. Then, she turned to Barbatos and stated, "Hey, watch your words. Zagan isn't feeling too tolerant right now."

"Oh please. Do you know how many times he's almost killed me?" Barbatos casually replied. In a certain sense, it was impressive that he never thought of changing his attitude despite all that. However, Nephteros curiously tilted her head to the side, confused by the turn of events.

"Why are you so angry? Because he listened in on your conversation? But what's so bad about that? Both of you seemed to be having a lot of fun when you were brushing Nephelia's head..." Nephteros inquired. And that, in turn, made Zagan and Nephy cover their faces and collapse on the spot.

"Lady Nephteros, it would be better if you did not talk of such things in front of the people in question," Richard, the young Angelic Knight, spoke up to correct her.

"Huh? Why? Is it immoral?"

"Um, no, not exactly, but, um..." Richard stumbled over his words. He didn't seem like a bad person, but his common sense was clearly ineffective when faced with dragons, elves, and sorcerers. And sensing that, Foll decided to step in.

"Zagan and Nephy are shy. They're embarrassed that other people saw all that, so you can't point it out."

"Hm... I see. I'll keep it in mind."

Unfortunately, having their daughter thoroughly explain the situation only served to cause both of them more mental trauma.

"Are you interested in the things they're doing?" Foll asked.

"A little. I kind of want to know what it's like," Nephteros responded with those words and an honest nod as she gazed at Zagan and Nephy.

Cut it out! At that point, Zagan wanted to just curl up into a ball and die.

"You're trying to speak more like an adult now, aren't you?" Nephteros asked as she cast a searching gaze over at Foll.

"Mhm. I'm the big sister now, so I have to!" Foll exclaimed. Zagan found the way his daughter thrust out her chest in pride extremely childish. However, Nephteros didn't seem to question it at all. Instead, she merely cupped her hands in front of her body in a pensive manner.

"You mean the mind grows alongside the body? That doesn't really seem to be the case with me, though..."

"Nope. That's wrong. Zagan said that adults think things through from different perspectives, which probably means we're supposed to see things from other points of view. Zagan obviously can't do that anymore, since he just did that with Nephy out of the blue, so I need to step up in his place."

"Urgh..." Zagan groaned as his consciousness faded because of her relentless barrage. He knew she had no ill will, but it was still a tough pill to swallow.

"I see. It really does seem like I have a lot left to learn," Nephteros muttered helplessly.

"A-Anyway! If what Selphy said is true, there should be people living here. Let's start by asking around," Zagan said as he used sorcery to improve his vision and spotted several structures near the temple. That was likely where the sirens lived.

"Zagan. We stand out a lot. We'll look suspicious," Foll pointed out.

"There's no need to worry. The conference is a perfect excuse. There should be plenty of outsiders here, so it won't look strange if we're wandering around," Zagan stated as he shook his head with an air of composure.

"This whole thinking from other perspectives thing is... really hard," Foll claimed as her shoulders drooped in disappointment.

"No, it's important to think of potential risk as well. You made a good point."

"Really?" Foll asked as her cheeks flushed despite his rather blunt words.

"Yes, really," Zagan answered. And after that, he said, "Well then, it's decided. Let's explore this place. Are you fine with that, Nephteros?"

Nephteros was Zagan's sister-in-law, not his subordinate, so he had no right to order her around.

"Got it, Zag..."

"What?"

"Now that I think of it, what should I call you?" Nephteros wondered, clearly confused. To her, Zagan was a sorcerer of a higher rank, a former enemy, a current guardian, and a brother-in-law. She was likely confused by all that conflicting information.

"Call me whatever you want. But as I said before, spare me any formalities."

"Then... Big Bro."

When she said that, everyone present was shocked to their core. They stared at her in wonder, trying to desperately unravel her thought process.

"...What?"

"No, um... Well, whatever. I suppose that's fine."

What is this? I'm getting the exact same strange feeling I do when Foll calls me daddy... At any rate, it definitely wasn't unpleasant, so Zagan simply nodded back at her despite how embarrassed he felt.

"So... why are you tagging along, Barbatos?" Zagan inquired. He followed them as they set off for the siren town, so their party currently consisted of Zagan, Nephy, Foll, Nephteros, her escort Richard, and Barbatos.

I need to return to my original body before my date with Nephy... Zagan didn't believe that Barbatos would be of any use, so he wanted him gone. And he felt especially strongly about it, since this could've been a family trip of sorts if not for his intrusion.

"That cat lady's over there, so it'll be fine. Actually, I can't even get close to Chastille when she's around, so I've got no choice but to kill time over with you," Barbatos stated as he let out a laugh and brushed back his unkempt hair.

"Hm...? Well, whatever."

Barbatos was speaking in an irritated tone, but Zagan couldn't really tell if he just hated Kuroka, or if he was mad he couldn't be by Chastille's side.

No, wait... Can't it be both? Zagan began to think something had changed about Barbatos. And based on their interaction earlier, Chastille didn't seem wholly dissatisfied with him, so what could it all mean? He was rather curious, but he knew he had to put his own romance first.

As they closed in on a road that was still some distance from the temple, the party came across an area covered in something that appeared to be green snow.

It looked to be a bronzed green color. And, of course, it wasn't really snow, but actually fragments of green moss-like debris that was scattered about in the area. Upon stepping into it they left a footprint behind and scattered the debris into the air. It truly resembled snow more than anything else.

Since sirens simply swam around, the clumps of debris always remained as they were. And so, though there was no debris near the buildings, there was plenty of it at their feet.

This is… sand? No, it's the remains of living beings… Zagan thought as he tried scooping some up in his hand. There was no smell of rot, but the irregular fragments looked more like fragmented bones than grains of sand. And, at the same time, he could see that they weren't in fact green, but white. Zagan looked up overhead, and though it was faint, some sunlight streamed down. It seemed the color of light that could reach them was limited, so at that depth, they largely only had green light, which was what tricked them into thinking the debris was green.

The houses around them were likely originally constructed using processed stones, but now they were covered in debris, barnacles, and seaweed, and the individual stones could no longer be distinguished. A faint light came out from the openings in the hundreds of dome-shaped buildings that were spread out before him. It was a fantastical sight that made one think countless glowing fish were floating about.

"Hm… It's unexpectedly beautiful, isn't it?" Zagan mumbled to himself.

"Yes. I think so as well," Nephy added as she nodded along, seemingly in a good mood.

If taking a walk through a special place is considered a date, then this may be one... Though, there were several others around them, which kind of ruined the mood. Still, Zagan was honestly happy as long as it pleased Nephy. And, as they gazed at that scenery, he suddenly heard Barbatos' voice.

"Hey, Zagan."

His voice wasn't resonating in the air. Instead, it felt more like it was ringing inside his head. And so, Zagan squinted his eyes for a moment, but immediately realized its nature and replied.

"Telepathic communication? When exactly did you learn this, Barbatos?"

It was sorcery that allowed people to communicate with another via thought. However, it wasn't as simple as it sounded. Though imperfect, it meant meddling with the thoughts of another person. If the gap in power was too large, or if the sorcerer didn't specialize in the field, it wouldn't even activate. And as a result, Zagan was unable to use it himself.

However, Barbatos failed at both those conditions, yet somehow succeeded in communicating telepathically with Zagan. Such a feat would have been impossible a mere half a year ago, so it seemed he was building up strength in his own way.

The fact that he's going out of his way to use it means he doesn't want the others overhearing us, right? Zagan realized his intent and awaited his reply quietly.

"Who cares. Listen, there's something I want to check. It's about Bifrons," Barbatos relayed that message in an irritated voice. In a surprising turn, it appeared Barbatos was using telepathy out of consideration for Nephteros. Bifrons was no longer able to appear

before Nephteros because Zagan cast sorcery on that Archdemon to force them into a covenant. Considering the fact that Bifrons was also an Archdemon, it may have been possible for them to eventually break it, but there were no signs of that occurring thus far.

"*What about Bifrons?*"

"*...Were you serious about what you said in the end?*"

Zagan knit his brows. He didn't remember saying anything all that strange at the time, but it seemed Barbatos thought differently.

"*I'm talking about how Bifrons fell in love with Nephteros. Is a monster like that capable of human emotions?*"

The only one who witnessed the conclusion to Zagan's confrontation with Bifrons was Barbatos. And his doubts regarding that matter weren't entirely unfounded. If Bifrons didn't love Nephteros, then the punishment Zagan bestowed upon the Archdemon wouldn't have been a punishment at all. And yet, Zagan started to reply instantly, as if it weren't all that big a deal.

"*Those words were a simple poison. When people have something pointed out to them, they start seeing it more.*"

"*Huh? Then, that was all a bluff? You a fucking idiot or something?*" Barbatos exclaimed as he began to chastise Zagan in an angry tone before getting cut off.

"*Nope. Bifrons is in love with Nephteros. However, if they weren't aware of that fact, it wouldn't have been much of a punishment. That's what I mean by my words being a poison.*"

"*I don't really think that's the case, though...*" Barbatos insisted that it was completely worthless, which irritated Zagan.

"*I granted Nephteros sorcery that could kill Bifrons. Having said that, it was something I threw together on the spot, so that Archdemon could have easily dismantled it.*"

It used a simplified Heaven's Scale to send Bifrons' head flying, but it wasn't enough to kill them. Still, it wasn't like Bifrons didn't experience the pain.

"And yet, Bifrons remained quiet and simply took it. I'm guessing that seeing Nephteros delighted over accomplishing something she thought impossible made Bifrons happy, so they allowed it."

"And that's why you think Bifrons is in love? Isn't that a stretch?"

"You may be right. However, the reason I'm so confident is because after Nephteros found out about the truth, Bifrons never tried to kill her directly."

"Yeah, killing someone you're in love with would be pretty messed up…" Barbatos mumbled. The fact that he truly believed that showed that he may have actually been a good person at heart.

"Bifrons could have ended Nephteros' life at any moment, yet they never even tried. Or rather, Bifrons couldn't. I'd guess that Bifrons was trying to get Nephteros to return after cornering her. But unfortunately, she ended up running away all the way into my domain."

It wasn't clear whether Bifrons was aware of any of their own conduct back then, but even that Archdemon should have understood that it wasn't worth making an enemy out of Zagan.

"Are there any idiots out there who would pick a fight with someone they couldn't defeat in their own domain? Bifrons dared to challenge me in my domain after losing on the boat, which meant they had no other choice."

That was because Bifrons knew he would try to save Nephteros. And if that happened, Bifrons would never get her back. That was why they could only desperately struggle to eke out a victory.

"Bifrons had no time, no hands to play, no chance at victory, and paid no attention to their own appearance while attempting to reclaim her. No one would ever do all that for a mere tool. I'm certain that *was only possible because deep down, Bifrons felt she was the most important thing in their life."*

That was why Zagan was convinced Bifrons was in love with Nephteros. And, since Bifrons wasn't even aware of that, he used poisonous words to harm the Archdemon.

"A crazy asshole can fall in love with someone..." Barbatos seemed to almost sound scared of believing him.

"It's not all that strange, is it? The longer you live alone, the lonelier you feel. Bifrons was always alone, so after experiencing the comfort of someone's company for the first time, it was only natural that they fell in love."

And yet, despite being fully aware of that fact, Zagan stole Nephteros. An Archdemon's retribution was truly cruel.

"..." Barbatos didn't say anything more, but oddly enough, Zagan couldn't sense any sort of denial from him. And just like that, he closed the telepathic link between them. When Zagan glanced over to Barbatos, who was right behind him, he saw him scratching his head in a conflicted manner.

That reaction... Is he really...? Zagan faintly believed it to be the case already, but it seemed Barbatos was now aware of it as well.

"Is something wrong, Master Zagan?" Nephy asked as she noticed the mix of sympathy and bewilderment on Zagan's face.

Zagan lowered his voice and whispered in reply.

"Oh... Um, last time, he asked me for some advice with his love life, so I was just thinking of how to reply," Zagan lowered his voice and whispered in reply.

"My... Lord Barbatos really is the serious type in that regard," Nephy muttered even as the tips of her ears turned slightly red.

Seems everyone knows your secret already, Barbatos...

Just this once, Zagan cheered on his undesirable friend.

163

Though they were walking around in the middle of town, perhaps because of Barbatos' appearance, they were unable to find a single person.

It doesn't seem like away... Speaking of rustling clothes seemed strange underwater, but Zagan could hear people stirring about and breathing from within the houses. However, they all seemed to be on guard and were only watching from a distance. It may have been that sirens were a very cautious race. Zagan stood around, clearly troubled over how to ask for help when he suddenly heard a suspicious voice.

"Heeheeheehee... How surprising. This is truly surprising. To think the day would come where I would meet you once more."

Behind me? Zagan turned around to confront the intruder.

"Hello, Silver-Eyed King."

However, the one standing before him was a small girl. She looked to be about the same age as Zagan's current form, if not a little older. At most, she was twelve or thirteen. She was likely the daughter of one of the participants at the conference, since she had two feet, which meant she wasn't a siren. Additionally, her golden hair was tied up on both sides, and her eyes were like a golden moon. She also wore a black dress that was covered in frills, and she carried an eccentric looking stuffed toy in her thin arms.

Her hair and her clothes gave off an impression that reminded him of Lilith. However, the stuffed toy in her arms was the most eye-catching thing about her. It looked almost... undead. There were thick threads intentionally hanging off it, revealing the areas where it had been patched up. In a way, it was unique, though creepy felt like the more appropriate term. In any case, Zagan didn't recognize the girl at all.

"What do you want?" Zagan asked. It would have been fine to ignore her, but he stopped because she was the first person he'd managed to meet in the area.

Silver-Eyed King... I think Lilith mentioned that name just earlier... Zagan's eyes were also supposedly silver, though probably closer to blue or gray. Either way, it wasn't proof of him belonging to some special species. Sure, it was rare, but it didn't have any value the way elves or dragons did. In any case, this girl may have been someone who possessed power, which meant there was the possibility that she could assist in dispelling Zagan's curse.

"Heeheehee, just like this child, your eyes are like lovely shells," the young girl claimed as she stretched her hand out toward Zagan in a longing manner. Upon closer inspection, it became clear that the stuffed toy's eyes were made of shells that were shaped like big buttons.

"What are you talking about? I don't know you."

Feeling somewhat creeped out, Zagan took a step back. However, the young girl paid no mind to that at all, and drew in even closer.

"Even so, I know you... How nostalgic. How very, very nostalgic. Why, it's so nostalgic that I feel like indulging myself and sucking you up right here."

That was when Zagan realized the young girl who was forming an unbecoming suspicious smile had two fangs sticking out of her mouth.

"You're... part of the Night Clan?"

Vampires, No Life Kings, Nosferatu. They were inhuman existences who had all sorts of detestable names. They were once human, but due to some unknown reason, they became detached from the circle of life and death. They were the most abominable beings in the world. And, at the same time, they were the very personification of the aspiration of all sorcerers, immortality. That was why sorcerers referred to them with respect as the Night Clan.

However, because they were even more heretical than sorcerers, the church thoroughly oppressed them. And since there weren't all that many of them to begin with, they practically vanished from the continent entirely. It seemed they had also escaped to Liucaon to survive... though it wasn't clear if that term was one fitting for those who knew naught of the concepts of life and death.

She isn't actually as young as she looks, huh?

"Oh, so you've finally remembered me, Silver-Eyed King," the girl of the Night Clan's bright red lips twisted into a smile as she said that.

"...No, I'm telling you that you have the wrong person. My name is—"

"I'm fully aware of that. You are he who inherited Marchosias' sigil, the new Archdemon, Lord Zagan," the girl said that, then readjusted the position of the stuffed toy in her arm and lifted up the hem of her skirt with her other hand to curtsy.

Is she just being a buffoon despite knowing all that? Zagan raised his guard as he mulled over such thoughts.

"In that case, why are you calling me Silver-Eyed King or whatev—!?" Zagan started questioning her, but the girl vanished from in front of his eyes.

She's gone? Zagan hadn't been careless, and yet, he lost sight of her entirely. That was a terrifying thought.

"Master Zagan!" Nephy screamed. And the moment he heard her voice, he felt a cold and wet sensation along his neck.

"But even so, the taste of your blood, your smell, and the color of your eyes are all the same..." the girl claimed. She had circled around directly behind Zagan instantaneously. And then, she began licking his neck with her bright red tongue.

Is she planning to suck my blood!? There were anecdotes that the Night Clan needed to suck the blood of others to maintain their existence. Zagan tried to shake her off, but her fingers were tightly clasped onto his shoulder, preventing any form of escape.

"Zagan doesn't like it. Stop!" Foll exclaimed as she grabbed the girl's head. Unfortunately, that just made the vampire gaze at Foll with her moon-like eyes.

"Oh my, I thought you were just a child with a large body, but it seems you're a proper babysitter. Good girl, good girl."

"...I feel like you're dangerous, so don't touch Zagan again," Foll ordered as she put more strength into her arm and tried to crush the girl's head. However, the girl's body crumbled away before she could.

"Heeheehee, how scary. I see. Even a young dragon is a threat. I'm starting to fear for my life," the girl stated as her body broke down into a countless number of bats, then reconstructed itself in the air.

"Then, you should just die," Foll said as she stood in front of the newly released Zagan. And then, she swung her arm and wove countless magic circles in its path. Upon seeing those magic circles, Zagan suddenly turned pale.

Hold on... What's with this number of circuits!? Zagan, who possessed the ability to devour sorcery, could see through the number of circuits woven into sorcery in an instant. Each magic circle Foll wove together had nearly ten thousand circuits within them, which was ridiculous. Heaven's Phosphor, which Zagan was reluctant to teach to Foll, had a little less than ten thousand circuits, but here she was putting together tens of thousands of circuits in an instant.

In her current form, Foll could easily manipulate the Dragon Form and the Five Fold Grand Flower.

Before long, the magic circles piled up into three locations. They looked just like the frame of an enormous cannon. And in truth, that was exactly what they were.

"Vanish," Foll muttered. And as she did, the three piles of magic circles let loose three distinct vivid lights. One let loose a severe heat ray that boiled the water and even burned the steam into nothing. One was a Borealis that froze over even the burned atmosphere itself and smashed it to bits. And the last was a hammer of lightning that could change the shape of a mountain.

Each one was a bundle of destruction that far surpassed what Foll's breath could normally manage, yet all three of them were being used along a precise single line that didn't even let a single small electrical discharge escape. They advanced, then eventually swallowed the vampire, but...

"Heeheeheehee, how violent. Dragons should show more restraint," the girl stated as she floated about casually.

She didn't dodge it... Did she block...? No, that's impossible, which means... Zagan let his thoughts run wild before arriving at the answer.

"I see. Members of the Night Clan are both here and not here at the same time."

It was much like how the moon would not break because someone threw a pebble at its reflection in a lake. Zagan's group was only witnessing a mirage, so there was no purpose in destroying it.

An Archdemon from a certain age referred to them as calamities with a will. Even if someone managed to destroy their bodies, they would not die, for they possessed no concept of death. Additionally, if one stabbed a stake through their heart and burned them to less than ash, they would only cease existing in the world for but a mere moment. Given time, they would appear again.

Preparing for a calamity could help minimize damages, but it could never actually prevent it, and the same could be said of the Night Clan.

"Oh my. Your silver eyes see through everything, but I can't really admire someone who's revealing a lady's secret," the girl confirmed what he said without showing any signs of hiding it, but Foll didn't seem to understand the meaning of her words.

"What a weird power... I don't know what it is, but is this enough to kill you?" Foll inquired. She appeared to be getting worked up by the vampire's provocative behavior. And so, she opened her mouth and took in a huge breath.

"Stop that, Foll! If you unleash your breath now, you'll blow away the town!"

"..." Foll remained silent. However, she surely noticed that fact herself.

Foll can't control her power right now... She had suddenly acquired the body and power of an adult. At first, she faltered at the simple task of just walking around, so there was no way she could control her mana like that. The triplex sorcery she used just now was splendidly accurate, but that was because she didn't even bring out half of her power. If she were to go all out, especially using her dragon's breath, it was plain as day what would happen.

And so, Foll reluctantly withdrew the breath that she was preparing to unleash. It seemed the girl from the Night Clan foresaw that Zagan would stop her, as she didn't show any signs at all of being perturbed.

"Could you not get so angry? All I did was come here to give you a small warning, since you've traveled so far to get here."

"Does that mean you're a participant of the elder's conference?" Zagan asked, probing for the meaning behind her words.

"It is fine for you to believe so."

"Huh? She's part of the Night Clan, right? Why would someone who doesn't even have to worry about surviving care about the extinction of other races?" Barbatos chimed in, sounding rather confused.

"...Oh my, that vulgar, perishable, sack of meat can speak?" the young girl replied as she stared at him with a vexed look in her eyes.

"You picking a fight!?" Barbatos roared in anger.

"Stop it, Barbatos. You were in the wrong there," Zagan said as he let out a sigh. Members of the Night Clan still had feelings, after all. Even Zagan could tell that Barbatos' little remark would touch a nerve.

"So? I'm certain you didn't approach me to anger Foll, so what's your business here?" Zagan inquired with a tired look in his eyes.

"Hm, I wonder... I am one who is disconnected from the cycle of life and death. A simple onlooker. I can do naught to those who possess life," the girl claimed as she laughed evasively, then muttered, "...Even a thousand years ago, all I did was watch."

"A thousand years ago...?"

What exactly did those words imply?

Raphael's been dreaming of something from back then as well... What happened during that time period?

"Oh, that's right. A warning. I came to give you a warning. I apologize. This has been so nostalgic and fun that I unintentionally forgot about it."

"A warning?"

"Yes. If you wish to be rewarded, you should first listen to the demands of others."

And, as if that were a signal, he heard the sound of loud footsteps drawing closer.

"Hang on! What's with this uproar!?" Lilith ran straight up to them and started demanding answers. It seemed that she came to check on the town after hearing that trouble was brewing.

Well, they could probably see Foll's sorcery from the temple... And that was when Zagan finally realized the truth. The vampire girl had caused this uproar to draw Lilith here. She just had to provoke them and make one of Zagan's companions go wild to draw her attention. And, if that still weren't enough, she just needed to talk in a roundabout manner to buy time. It was a brilliant plan, which had already worked before Zagan even realized her intentions.

"Hey, the rich brat over there. What's going on here?" Lilith asked as she faced Zagan.

"...You know who that is, don't you?" Zagan asked as he pointed to the girl who was floating above them.

"Huh? What are y— Eeek! Lady Alshiera! Why are you here!?" Lilith shrieked, going completely stiff as she turned toward the vampire.

Her strong-willed face was dyed with terror, and the girl named Alshiera simply laughed as if she found her response strange.

"Oh my, if it isn't my cute little fawn. I see that you've come all the way out here just to meet me. Should I be giving you a reward?"

"Th-Th-Th-Th-Th-Th-That would be unthinkable! I c-c-can't receive a reward from such an awe-inspiring ally!" Lilith responded in a meek manner as she was trembling so vigorously that it was pitiful.

Guess she's also involved with this woman... Well, she was a monster who went unscathed after being attacked by Foll. Lilith wasn't even a sorcerer, so it was no wonder that the poor succubus didn't dare to oppose her. And, since her personality was so easy to understand, it was clear that Lilith was a victim who was dragged here on the vampire's whim.

"Hey, does this girl really know that much?" Zagan asked as he clicked his tongue and stood in front of Lilith.

"Heehee, I'm so happy that you catch on quick. My cute little fawn here is quite clever. This child possesses the answer to your question, and if she can't answer you, then you won't find your answer here," the vampire stated that with a laugh, as if enjoying the beginning of a fun play. And Zagan, in turn, looked back at her with a plainly displeased expression.

You want me to ask this annoying girl...? He hated the idea, but oddly enough, he didn't feel like the vampire was lying... Well, having said that, it also didn't sound like she was telling the truth, either.

"Well, fine. I'll believe you, but there's one thing I don't get. What the hell do you have to gain from this?"

"Hey, calm down! You can't talk to her like that! You'll experience something worse than death if you don't stop!" Lilith exclaimed. And after Zagan pushed back Lilith, who tugged at his clothes with a pale face, the vampire let out another playful laugh.

"Isn't it human nature to want to make something fun even more amusing?"

Zagan was astonished and dumbfounded by the fact that a being who was undead could talk about human nature.

"Well then, I shall bid you adieu, my beloved Silver-Eyed King, and... Azazel."

"What!?" Lilith exclaimed, clearly confused by her choice of words.

"Azazel..." Zagan muttered. Why did she mention that name? He wanted to know more, but unfortunately, the girl turned into a colony of bats and flew off.

She had just mentioned the name of the Thirteenth Sacred Sword Zagan was looking into. Though, he'd also discovered that it was the name of the dark side of the church. And yet, the vampire just used it like the name of a person even though the only member of Azazel in the area was Kuroka, who wasn't even present. Nothing made any sense.

"...Tch, the hell was she?" Zagan asked as he clicked his tongue in irritation.

"That's no good! If you get involved with that person... with Lady Alshiera, you'll get some unreasonable demand forced on you, and if you don't carry it out to the letter, you'll go through hell..."

It seemed she was Lilith's boss... or rather, someone of higher status than her. Though, based on her reaction, it was clearly not something that could be summed up that simply.

But... Lilithiera... Alshiera... On top of their names being similar, even their clothing and hairstyles matched. Zagan didn't believe a haughty girl like Lilith would copy the looks of someone she detested, so...

"Isn't she one of your allies?"

"Give me a break! That person just enjoys watching us squirm... Oh, I don't think she hates us or anything, though..."

What's with this? I'm being reminded of Gremory and Manuela here... Lilith's reaction was similar to that of the girls those two teased into submission. That was why Zagan could tell that Lilith was someone unfortunate that Alshiera was interested in. And in that case...

"Was she referring to you when she said Azazel?"

"Huh? She wasn't... I think. That person always speak in riddles, so it's better not to worry about it. I mean, she even called you the Silver-Eyed King... Wait..." Lilith suddenly trailed off and peered in at Zagan's face.

"Hold on... Are your eyes maybe... silver?"

Zagan was wondering how she hadn't noticed already, but then he realized they were at the bottom of the ocean. Colors were all muddled to non-sorcerers down here, so it wouldn't have been odd if she didn't notice.

"You have a problem with that?" Zagan asked as he brushed Lilith aside with a grimace. Thinking back, he realized that during his childhood, when he performed highway robbery, his fellow waifs kept their distance from him because they found his eyes creepy. And so, he didn't like it when others focused on that aspect of him.

"You're kidding… Why would Lady Alshiera call this kid by that name…? Hey, wait. Zagan… was it? Why are you even here?" Lilith started questioning his motives as she shrank back in shock.

Zagan knew she would refuse to answer his questions if he didn't respond, so he let out a sigh of resignation and relented.

"You should at least remember the names of the guests you've invited. I'm Archdemon Zagan, Marchosias' successor."

Upon hearing that, Lilith froze on the spot for a short while, then turned completely pale and collapsed with a thud.

"So after that, you ended up coming here?"

Unable to just leave Lilith as she was after she collapsed, Zagan's group ended up reluctantly heading over to the temple where the elder's conference was being held, then proceeded to what appeared to be a waiting room within the temple. Unlike the outside, the room was fully furnished, and more importantly, it was filled with air instead of water. There wasn't anything like a bed, but the space was large enough to fit a few dozen people and even had sofas from the surface. There were several bright lamps set up around the room, which meant there wasn't a blue shade cast over everything for once. This was likely done out of consideration for all the other races. Even if they could breathe, those who lived on the surface would feel more at ease when in a place filled with air.

Zagan's group of six, as well as Chastille's group of Angelic Knights, sat around. Further in the corner were Kuroka, Selphy, and Lilith, who was still quite pale in the face. And, when Chastille spoke, seemingly out of pity for the poor girl, Zagan replied with a sour look.

"...It seems nothing is going my way anymore. Is this form to blame?" Zagan inquired.

"Well, if it is, isn't this a good opportunity to get some help from Nephy and the others? Normally, you're too strong, so they never get the chance to assist you," Chastille replied. Upon getting scolded by Chastille of all people, Zagan grimaced.

"That's none of your business. The idea that I'll grow by being saved is silly, and something only the helpless would ever believe," Zagan reflexively responded in a strong tone, which made Chastille look down with a sad gaze. Zagan was aware that he was irritatingly venting his anger, but he believed it was that vampire Alshiera's fault for messing with him earlier.

My mind might be getting influenced by my body's transformation... That was what had happened in Nephy's case, anyway. Back when Zagan was ten years old, he hated everything in the world, and he made that clear to any observers.

"Lord Archdemon. Lady Chastille was only saying that out of consideration. That is one of her virtues. Please choose your words more wisely," Richard cut into the conversation, unable to let Zagan's words fly. He surely had no ill intent either. However, his words still grated on Zagan's nerves. And, as Zagan tried to open his mouth to speak, he was suddenly embraced from behind.

"It's alright. Master Zagan is simply bad at expressing himself. I assure you, he isn't making light of Chastille," Nephy stated. It seemed she was the one who had embraced him. And even while hugging Zagan lovingly, she continued, "But, if we are to choose our words more wisely, then you should as well. Please don't speak of 'virtues,' Sir Angelic Knight. One person's virtues... can be another's curse. For example, if someone decided to act and hurt a 'cursed child' because 'there's a child here who's been afflicted by her poison...'"

There were those who acted innocent, hurt others, then tried to save them to appear 'virtuous.' Such people let their delusions run wild to the point where they tried to impose their wills on others and oppress them. And the most dreadful part was that they truly believed they were doing a good thing. They didn't doubt that for a second. That was why Zagan hated selfish and irresponsible people who prattled on about their virtues or being virtuous.

"I've experienced such things in the past, and I believe Master Zagan has suffered even more, so please don't speak of virtues in a relaxed manner," Nephy stated flatly. She had been oppressed in the hidden elven village for sixteen years. She saw such repulsive things there that she had lost her emotions. That was exactly why she could understand Zagan's pain. And, perhaps because she got through to him, Richard bit down on his lips and bowed his head.

"I was out of line. Please forgive me."

"...Sorry, I made you say something unpleasant," Zagan said as he looked over to Nephy with a pained expression on his face.

"Don't be. I assure you, you're as wonderful in this form as ever, Master Zagan."

"Well, it's certainly true that there are people I can rely on here," Zagan muttered as he scratched his cheek. It seemed he could no longer remain offended by the idea of accepting help.

"Please don't forget that I'm also someone who's more than willing to assist you," Chastille proclaimed as she smiled at him in relief.

"Well, I think that goes for most people here..." Nephteros added on. Zagan simply shrugged his shoulders when he heard his sister-in-law's words. And as he did, Lilith finally recovered and stood up.

"Lilith, are you alright?" Kuroka called out to her in a worried voice.

"I'm fine. There's no way a Hypnoel would go into shock over something like this!" Lilith replied. Her knees were still trembling with a clatter, but the succubus puffed out her chest even as her face spasmed. Then, she looked over to Zagan and asked, "So, are you really an Archdemon?"

"I may look small right now, but that is what they call me."

Lilith grimaced as if she wasn't fully convinced, but nobody else was denying it, so she couldn't do anything but accept reality. And eventually giving up, she kneeled on the spot.

"Then, newly crowned and esteemed Archdemon, allow me to ask you this as the succubus Lilithiera who represents the elders. Why did you not meet the elders despite being here?"

"There's no need to be so polite. I've never bothered with courtesy, so I don't expect it from anyone else," Zagan said. Some of those present were making a 'Huh, really?' face, but that didn't really matter.

"Then... I'll take you up on that offer, but I still want an answer. Are you the same as Lord Marchosias? Or not?" Lilith looked somewhat troubled by his words, but she still stood back up as she asked that question.

Marchosias...? Zagan raised his brow when he heard that. His name didn't seem to come up because Zagan had inherited his sigil. Did that Archdemon do something in these lands?

"The answer to that is clear. I'm different from Marchosias. To be honest, I've never even met him, so I know nothing of what he did to you."

Zagan had inherited his Sigil of the Archdemon from Marchosias, but he certainly didn't want anyone to blame him for his actions.

"It looks like you're misunderstanding something here. Lord Marchosias was a great person. He was the one who sheltered us races who were on the path to extinction," Lilith explained as she stared at him with a blank look on her face.

"Sheltered...? An Archdemon helped? Are you sure you're talking about an Archdemon, the most heinous of sorcerers?" Zagan asked. That was a valid question. Most races were on the verge of extinction because of sorcerers, so the worst of the lot helping them was unheard of.

Why was Marchosias' name following him around when Zagan was running about trying to find a way to dispel his curse? Nothing in his legacy had to do with dispelling curses...

"Are you different? I haven't heard the full details yet, but didn't you save Kuroka and Selphy?" Lilith inquired as she cocked her head to the side. It seemed she was informed of some details by her friends.

Ugh, why did they mention that...? Zagan averted his gaze from Lilith out of embarrassment.

"I was just concerned about Kuroka because she's a relative of one of my subordinates, and Selphy just happened to meet Nephy. Do I look like some softhearted fool who would save total strangers?" Zagan said haughtily, but Selphy sprang to her feet in an instant and raised her hand.

"Objection! Mister Zagan saved me when it looked like I was about to get eaten by a monster! On top of that, he got, like, really hurt and didn't even say a thing!"

"I also have an objection. He saved me from slavers before even knowing I was related to Lord Raphael. There was nothing in it for him at the time."

Both Selphy and Kuroka objected, and eventually, even Chastille and Nephteros joined the bandwagon.

"Then, I'll also object. Leaving an Angelic Knight of the church like me alive should have been nothing but a hindrance, yet Zagan has saved me several times over."

"Me too... Um, where do I even start? I can't even list it all..."

I'm begging you guys to keep quiet! Zagan wanted to yell at them all, but his voice had been killed by the shame. And, as he covered his face, Foll couldn't help it anymore and spoke in his stead.

"Zagan is shy. Don't say any more," Foll interjected to make that statement. His daughter's response was needlessly painful, and it only managed to make Lilith laugh.

"Well, it certainly does look like you're different from Lord Marchosias. This is the first time I've seen someone who's the exact opposite of Selphy."

"You're, like, totally right. It's like I'm looking at you, Lilith."

"Erk..." Lilith groaned. Her thoughtless comment was mercilessly thrown right back at her, which made Lilith pin down her flat chest as she writhed in agony. Sensing nothing would progress at this rate, Zagan mustered his willpower and lifted his face, at which point he noticed something.

Lilith is... trembling? Lilith's fists, which were down at her sides, were trembling slightly. She was likely terrified now that she knew Zagan was an Archdemon. Looks be damned, there was no way she wasn't scared. And yet, she still wished to speak. That fact filled Zagan with interest.

"...Hmm. You're free to think whatever you like, but what is it you want of me?" Zagan inquired.

"It's about our pact with Lord Marchosias... I'd like you to succeed it," Lilith answered after she got her breathing in order.

"Hmm... I don't really get it. Marchosias wasn't an Archdemon who indulged in meaningless slaughter, but I'm certain he wasn't a philanthropist either, so why did he end up protecting races like yours?"

It seemed like the answer to his question would be rather long, so Zagan snapped his fingers and used sorcery to pull in one of the chairs around them. Lilith was the only one who was standing. She stared at the chair unexpectedly for a moment, but plunked down into the seat.

"Let's see... It's a rather long explanation. Is that alright?"

"I don't mind," Zagan firmly stated. And as if on cue, Lilith straightened herself out, then began speaking.

"First I think I should talk about the Silver-Eyed King. According to legends, about a thousand years ago, the world was on the verge of destruction due to a battle with a Grotesque God. And the one who saved us from that was the Silver-Eyed King. He used a tremendous amount of mana and ancient arms to slay the Grotesque God."

After saying that, Lilith suddenly pulled out something that looked like a small shield.

No... is that a mirror? It snugly fit in both her hands, and though it was made of metal, it was polished to such a fine degree that it reflected one's face perfectly. Mirrors were often used as tools in sorcery as well. Nowadays, it was common to use a film of tin or mercury on a glass sheet, but in the past they used polished metals or gems. Compared to glass, these were far more sturdy, and even now they remained useful.

"The Holy Treasures passed down in my house of Hypnoel, Kuroka's house of Adelhide, and Selphy's house of Neptunia, were the arms wielded by the Silver-Eyed King. It is said that our three great lines are his direct descendants."

"Hmm. Well, it's quite common for legacies to be passed down through one's bloodline…" Zagan mumbled. And on that topic, it was also natural for one's family to split into branches over a thousand year span.

Based on how spread out their races are, the Silver-Eyed King took in members of multiple races, huh? If it was something that involved their ancestors, then they couldn't just laugh off Alshiera's profound words.

"Lord Marchosias was a sworn friend of the Silver-Eyed King who fought by his side. That was why he protected Liucaon, the country of his descendants. It is said that we succubi and sirens have only managed to survive because we have the protection of an Archdemon," Lilith explained as she traced her finger along the surface of the mirror. Her focus seemed to be on Kuroka, who was sitting behind her. When Kuroka's people were attacked, Marchosias was still alive. In all likelihood, the sorcerers who attacked them received retribution. They were surely long dead, but nevertheless, the attack itself couldn't be prevented. It may have been that Marchosias was growing weak at the time.

Sworn friend… was that also the time Wise Dragon Orobas and Marchosias became sworn friends? Zagan thought as he shifted his gaze over to Foll. That was likely why they stood side by side in battle half a year ago. However, the problem was what exactly it was they fought against.

"As for records from a thousand years ago, there are few documents left even on the continent. In that case, some sort of incident that surpassed the differences between sorcerers, the church, and our races likely occurred," Zagan muttered to himself in an attempt to put his thoughts in order.

For example... the invasion of the Demon Lord... It felt like several threads were finally coming together.

"I don't know how it was passed down on the continent, but it's said that it was a tremendous battle that destroyed many countries and races. The Silver-Eyed King took the races who dwindled in that fight to Liucaon, and protected them with his Holy Treasures," Lilith expanded on her earlier words, then looked over to Selphy and said, "The continent has yet to tread into Liucaon because the sirens use their Holy Treasure to manipulate the ocean currents."

"Huh? Our Holy Treasure's, like, something that amazing?" Selphy, who was supposedly a princess, seemed surprised. It was almost like that was the first time she'd ever heard that fact.

"I see... Then isn't there no need for an Archdemon's protection?" Zagan commented with a nod.

"We are not so arrogant as to believe we can protect our country and all its people with just three Holy Treasures. If that was possible, Kuroka's people would not have perished..." Lilith replied, then looked straight into Zagan's eyes and stated, "We require a stronger power to ensure our survival. It's been said that you passed judgment on two other Archdemons, so we're willing to do anything to ensure your protection."

I see... They've decided this after analyzing the whole situation... Zagan's eyes widened when he came to that conclusion. It seemed he was thought of as a special existence even among the Archdemons thanks to his battles with Bifrons and Orias, so there weren't any sorcerers out there who would risk incurring his wrath. And that was exactly why Lilith made that request of him in such a straightforward manner.

She also knows of loneliness... He felt like he understood why she was willing to go so far despite her fear. One of her two childhood friends fled their home and her whereabouts were unknown, and the other was believed to be dead. What sort of turbulent emotions could she have been feeling this whole time? Honestly, even Zagan couldn't begin to guess. And so, he decided he had to confirm something.

"Well, I understand what you're saying. By the way, under whose order were you assigned this role for negotiations?"

"Um, I wasn't... ordered by anyone... To be honest... the elders were supposed to ask you directly..." Lilith jumped with a start, and mumbled those words in response.

"In other words, you decided to speak sharply to me, an Archdemon, of your own accord?"

"I-I mean... you're saying you won't meet with the elders, and if I let you go here, we might never meet again, so..." Lilith's voice trailed off weakly as she started to feel like she did something she shouldn't have. And yet, Zagan replied with a smile.

"Very well. I like that. I'll take on your damn request."

"R-Really!?" Lilith exclaimed, her expression brightening up in an instant.

"However, I will not succeeded Marchosias' pledge. You've piqued my interest, so I'll be taking you along under my wing. I don't intend to protect total strangers."

"Th-That's no good! The others will be in danger if you don't agree to help!"

"What are you saying? I said I would take on your damn request. I'll lend you my name, so I won't complain no matter who you decide to protect with it."

"Uhhh…?" Lilith muttered. She couldn't follow his words, so Kuroka cut in to clear her bewilderment.

"In the end, it's all the same. If you and the others protect Liucaon, it'll be just like he is."

And finally coming to an understanding, Lilith let out a sigh of relief.

"I thank you for your consideration, Archdemon… but why do you have to say it in such a roundabout way?"

"Well, Mister Zagan's, like, all shy and stuff, just like you!"

This dumb fish… Should I just roast her for dinner? Zagan glared at Selphy spitefully, but the siren simply smiled and waved back at him like she didn't understand anything at all. Lilith was also glaring at Selphy in irritation, but she immediately calmed down and faced Zagan once more.

"Then, what would you have us give you to bind this pledge?"

Zagan was finally getting a chance to talk about what he came here for, so calmed down and nodded. Then, he glanced over at Nephy, who also nodded as if to cheer him on.

To think I'd be relieved by such a simple act…

"Me and my daughter are currently under the effects of a troublesome curse. I want the power and knowledge of Liucaon to dispel it," Zagan explained as he pointed over to Foll. That was the only reason he traveled to Atlastia. And upon hearing that request, Lilith's face stiffened up completely.

"Why do you think we can dispel a curse that an Archdemon can't?"

"You have those Holy Treasures or whatever, right? And even if it's only but a fragment, haven't you all inherited the powers of that Silver-Eyed King?"

"...Got it. I'll get the cooperation of the elders and we'll try everything in our power, but... don't expect too much from us, okay?" Lilith said after she hung her head down in thought for a while. And, leaving them with that, she ran off in a hurry.

Well, with this, I've finally accomplished my first goal... Zagan though as he sank back into the sofa. It would have been great if Lilith brought back some sort of clue with her.

"You did great today, Master Zagan," Nephy called out to him in a voice laden with admiration.

"Well, I'm sure everyone's worn out from it."

"Perhaps, but you've worked extremely hard. Good job."

Realizing that he was getting used to being treated like a child, Zagan became flustered on the inside. He then noticed that Foll had become quiet. His daughter was a person of few words, but the last conversation was focused on her, so she should've chimed in. However, she was simply staring up at the ceiling in a daze.

"Is something wrong, Foll?"

"...It's nothing."

Based on her reaction, Zagan had doubts, but he didn't prod because he was worried about annoying her. And so, he lost the opportunity to do so. Perhaps it was because he was in the body of the child. Or perhaps he was just worn out like Nephy implied. Either way, after relaxing, Zagan was overwhelmed by a sense of drowsiness, and fell asleep before he even knew it.

"Is Zagan asleep?"

The sirens had bedrooms prepared for their conference guests, so after Zagan fell asleep, Nephy laid him down in a bed. And, when she exited the room, she found Foll waiting for her.

"Yes. He was likely tired from the long trip. I must say, his sleeping face was so adorable…"

"…Nephy, you look happy."

"Th-That's not true!" Nephy shook her head in a fluster when her daughter teased her. Then, she admitted, "No, I may actually be happy."

"Nephy?" Foll tilted her head to the side, clearly confused.

"With Master Zagan as he is now, there's much we can do for him. He's finally relying on me, and you as well, Foll…" Nephy stated with a strained smile before saying, "…No. That's no good. Even though Master Zagan is troubled by this transformation, I'm saying I'm happy about his troubles."

"No… I get it…" Foll said as she crouched down in front of the door quietly and hugged her knees.

"Zagan told me he wanted me to stay a child. I feel like I get that just a bit now. If Zagan were an adult, he wouldn't get all angry or act spoiled like that."

The person in question had no intention of acting spoiled, but at times like when Nephy and Foll were overbearingly feeding him food, he told them what he wanted next. That was in part because Nephy and the others were pushing childish behavior onto him, but they were happy that he accepted that and acted to fit the part.

"Zagan and Nephy... You guys didn't have a time like that, but you can't turn back the clock. Right now, Zagan only looks like a child," Foll said in a sad voice, then let out a sigh and continued, "That's why he gave me what I wanted, since he knew I'd learn a lesson."

"In truth, you already knew that and didn't like it, right?" Nephy asked as she sat down next to her daughter.

"Yeah..." Foll replied as she buried her face into her knees. Then, she added, "Still, I was happy too. Really happy."

"It's alright. People have to go through things like this to become proper adults," Nephy explained as she began brushing her daughter's head. That was also the case for Nephy. Thinking about her past experiences and the lessons she'd learned because of them was painful, so she lived without feeling anything at all. However, upon meeting Zagan, she experienced more things that put her life into a greater perspective, acquired a daughter in Foll, and had many residents come to the castle. And yet, despite all that, she still felt herself lacking in the life experience department.

In the end, Nephy didn't believe herself to truly be an adult, but still, she felt like she was on the path to becoming one because of the many lessons she'd learned.

"Even though I've grown bigger, I'm still a child..." Foll muttered in a somewhat unconvinced tone.

"Yes. And I am one as well."

"You are?" Foll asked as she stared back at Nephy in wonder.

"Yes. For the longest time, all I did was cower without trying to learn a thing... But now, I can't remain a child..." Nephy explained. In the past, she let the elves in her village who oppressed her get slaughtered, and for some reason, she was the only one who survived.

It may have been better to save them... However, if she did that, her life would have remained the same, and she would never have met Zagan. That was why she never once thought of wanting to undo her decision. Even if she were faced with that instant once more, she would simply allow them to be slaughtered again. It may have been possible to save them, but the village wouldn't have remained if she did. And without the village, they would have eventually been discovered by humans, which would have resulted in the exact same outcome.

Nephy had decided to live while carrying that burden of the past. Without running away, she accepted it, carried it, properly faced forward, and marched on. That was the answer she arrived at after looking at her destroyed village. And, as a result, she couldn't just remain a child any longer. That was all there was to it.

"Then, was Zagan also forced to become an adult?" Foll cocked her head to the side as she asked that question.

"Yes. I'm sure that's the case... However, Master Zagan's situation was even more pressing..."

What Nephy and Zagan had in common was that they both had nobody who would save them. They were both utterly alone. Of course, there were those who loved loneliness. For example, people who desired solitude when exhausted by the crowds. However, that was different from what Nephy and Zagan experienced. What they felt was a pain called 'loneliness.' And when faced with it, Nephy decided to shut her heart entirely, while Zagan chose to grow strong. If he hadn't made that decision, he would have died. But unfortunately, he grew strong enough to fend off any and all distress without any effort, like a sword strong enough to cut straight through its own scabbard. Nephy believed this to be a truly saddening strength, which was why she wanted to become his scabbard. She wanted to become strong to help keep Zagan's strength in check so he could live a more normal life.

In that sense, I can truly understand Foll's feelings…

"I wonder… which I am… right now…" Foll muttered as she grabbed her own chest.

"Foll…" Nephy tried to call out to her when footsteps suddenly began approaching them from the hallway. She turned toward them and said, "Miss Lilith?"

It was the succubus. And, as Nephy called her name, she jumped up with a start.

Now that I think of it, I ended up threatening her earlier… The girl seemed rather arrogant, but that didn't excuse the fact that she treated her rather poorly.

"Oh, um, you're… Zagan's… lover? And daughter… right?" Lilith spoke to them as she began backing off timidly. Nephy became bashful upon being called his lover, and as she unintentionally covered her face, Lilith continued, "U-Um, I made the appeal… t-to have the curse investigated… The elders promised t-to pour their h-hearts into cooperating, s-so I think a response should c-come… soon…"

"Th-Thank you very much. Um, shorr… sorry about earlier."

"Are you pretending to be babies?"

Foll called them out despondently as she took in their constant stuttering.

"Um, I'll apologize if I'm wrong, but you're the daughter… right?" Lilith asked as she looked at Foll with a clear sense of confusion in her eyes.

"Mm. Zagan's my daddy."

"Y-You don't mean that in some indecent way, do you?"

"How could it be indecent?"

"You can use the word 'daddy' in an indecent manner?"

Foll stared back at Lilith blankly, and even Nephy didn't understand what she was saying either, so she cocked her head to the side.

"I-I-I-I-I-It's nothing!" Lilith exclaimed as she sealed her mouth in a fluster.

"If you say so... We talked about the curse earlier, correct? Foll was originally about the same age as Master Zagan appears now," Nephy answered that question that Lilith didn't even ask.

"Well, I heard that, but you're not human, are you? If you're his daughter despite being of a different race, does that mean you're adopted?"

"Yeah... I was left all alone after Father died, so Zagan became my daddy," Foll explained that with a nod in response to Lilith's puzzlement.

"You must be quite the rare species if an Archdemon has adopted you..."

"Yeah, I'm a dragon."

"Huh...?" Lilith froze up for a few moments, then continued, "Huh, a dragon? The ones who think of all living beings as prey and stand at the summit of all predators? The terrors of the sky who even send demons running? Those monsters on par with gods who can easily slaughter anything and everything? You mean that dragon?"

That description was ridiculous. Just what were dragons in this girl's mind? Foll then stood up and raised both her hands.

"Rawr, I'll eat youuu!" Foll roared as she stood up and raised both her hands.

"EEEEEEEEEEEEEEEEEEEEEEEEEEEEEEEK!" Lilith screamed, trembled violently, and tumbled down behind Nephy in response. And, after watching that reaction, Nephy looked over to Foll in wonder.

"Come now, Foll. Don't you feel sorry for teasing her?"

"I didn't think she would be so scared..." Foll mumbled. Lilith was still shuddering intensely behind Nephy.

"It's okay. Right now, I'm not hungry. I won't eat anyone."

"Th-There's something wrong with the way you put that!" Lilith screamed yet again, but she didn't seriously think that Foll was her enemy, so she peaked out nervously from behind Nephy's back.

"What kind of legends about dragons are passed down in Liucaon?" Nephy inquired.

"Let's see... For us, it's mainly the battle between Wise Dragon Orobas and Black Dragon Marbas. It was one of the stories written about in the Silver-Eyed King's adventures, but the greatness and the terror of dragons were passed along with that legend," Lilith explained as she raised her guard.

"I want to hear that one!" Foll demanded as she bent over in excitement upon hearing her father's name. At that, Lilith puffed out her chest with pride and pulled a small lyre out of nowhere.

"I-I suppose I have no other choice! Consider this an honor! My song is usually reserved for royalty!" Lilith proclaimed. Her attitude made it unclear whether she was doing this unwillingly or out of pure joy.

"Some time after the Silver-Eyed King defeated the Grotesque God, Black Dragon Marbas trampled over the lands of Liucaon. And so, our Silver-Eyed King set out to subjugate the beast. During his journey, he fluttered over ten mountains and strode over a hundred rivers, chasing the Black Dragon for a thousand miles. Eventually, he caught up, but by then his journey had lasted over a year."

Lilith's song wasn't so much a song as a tale accompanied by the melody of her lyre. It was a form of art that was starting to fade, much like Nephy's celestial mysticism and Selphy's singing.

Is this the reason Miss Alshiera told us to ask Miss Lilith about this matter? Regardless of the reason, Foll was listening to her attentively with sparkles in her eyes, which was good enough.

"And having reached the Black Dragon Marbas, our king grieved, 'Oooh, why Marbas!? Why would you, who fought valiantly by my side through many a battle, massacre innocents!?' For you see, the Silver-Eyed King and Black Dragon Marbas were sworn friends who fought the Grotesque God together."

The Black Dragon didn't reply, so they fought then and there. According to her song, the Silver-Eyed King tried to stop him, but Marbas was incredibly powerful, and the Silver-Eyed King could not bring himself to injure his former ally. The battle raged on for three days and three nights, ending in the Silver-Eyed King's defeat. However, Lilith's song did not end there.

"And so, the Black Dragon spoke, 'Oh, Silver Eyes. Your figure has become that of an unsightly beast. You'll do well to live on, trapped in that pitiful figure of yours. Poor, poor, Silver Eyes!' The Black Dragon cast a curse upon the king, and the king was transformed into a monster."

A curse that transforms one's figure... Nephy was startled upon hearing the word curse, but soon enough, gears started to turn in her head. Could that have been a clue on how to solve Zagan and Foll's issue?

"And thus, the one the king turned to was Wise Dragon Orobas. With the figure of a beast, the king was unable to descend upon human habitats, and his journey went on another three years."

It seemed it was finally time for Orobas' appearance. That knowledge made Foll straighten up and nod repeatedly.

"So the Wise Dragon spoke, 'Oh Silver Eyes, the only thing that can dispel thy curse is the kiss of a maiden who knows naught of impurity.' Alas, the king's figure was that of an unsightly beast! Who would love him as he was?"

After that, the Silver-Eyed King moved in accordance with Orobas' advice, and requested a kiss from a blind girl he saved and nurtured. However, when they drew close, she discovered that he was a beast. Luckily, the girl believed in the Silver-Eyed King and they exchanged a kiss, returning the king to his human form. Following that, he once more challenged Black Dragon Marbas alongside Wise Dragon Orobas.

"Straddling the back of the Wise Dragon, the king continued his struggle for seven days and seven nights. The two new allies found themselves heavily wounded, and just as their willpower waned, Orobas' fangs finally pierced Marbas' neck!"

Even as the battle reached its conclusion, Black Dragon Marbas remained alive. The Silver-Eyed King tried to save his life, but Marbas used the last of his power to launch an attack, so the king was forced to deliver the finishing blow with his sword. It was said that Marbas could no longer feel joy when moving from battle to battle, so he turned to committing atrocities to find new forms of pleasure. And when the Silver-Eyed King ended his reign of terror, Black Dragon Marbas thanked him as he breathed his last. The Silver-Eyed King came to fully realize that a stern hand was needed to guide his people, and the story ended with the king aspiring to be a leader who was both kind and strict.

It's a rather sad story... Even though the Silver-Eyed King and Black Dragon Marbas were the closest of friends, he was forced to murder him.

"Phew... H-How was that?" Lilith wiped away the sweat from her brow and smiled ear to ear as she finished her song.

"Wow... Father was cool."

"Huh? Father? What do you mean?" Lilith asked as she cocked her head to the side.

"Foll's father was the esteemed Wise Dragon Orobas who was in that song," Nephy replied with a strained smile.

"WHAT!?" Lilith jumped up in surprise, but Nephy didn't notice as she began absentmindedly staring off into the distance.

"Can a kiss... truly dispel a curse?"

"Well, it's quite a common occurrence in stories... There's also one about a prince who was turned into a frog returning to normal thanks to a kiss, and one about a sleeping beauty who was awoken by a kiss..."

"Zagan said that kisses are very special in sorcery," Foll added with a nod.

"I see... Unfortunately, I'm not very familiar with such stories."

"What a waste! Though, I'm also jealous!" Lilith exclaimed as she shook her head vigorously in grief.

"You're jealous of me?"

"Yeah! You get to enjoy the stories without any prior knowledge. Stories are more fun when you don't know the ending. There's nothing better than that."

I see. That's an interesting though. It's not one I would've had from my perspective, at least... Nephy swore to think of everything in an optimistic light, but it felt like her inexperience was being thrust before her.

If by some chance, a kiss can dispel a curse... Nephy tried touching her own lips as she had that thought. Then, she imagined Zagan's lips locking with hers.

How bold! Would Master Zagan... permit such an act...? Nephy's heart was beating like a drum. And noticing that, Lilith tilted her head to the side.

"Are you okay? Your ears are bright red."

"I-I'm fine!"

Logically, there was no way a curse that two Archdemons gave up on dispelling could be solved with a single kiss. If it was that easy, Zagan would have tested it out right away. And so, Nephy drove her wild delusions out of her head in a fluster.

"You are quite knowledgeable, Miss Lilith. Are most succubi very familiar with such songs?" Nephy questioned the girl to try and change the subject, but Lilith looked back at her with a somewhat bitter expression on her face.

"The songs of the succubi aren't all that special. Selphy's singing is far better, but..."

"Um, if it's something I should not pry into, then please forget I even asked," Nephy moved to withdraw her question when she felt the tension in the air, but Lilith shook her head.

"No. It's fine. How do I put it… It's because it's something Lady Alshiera taught me…"

Both Foll and Nephy stared at her in surprise upon hearing that.

"By Lady Alshiera, you mean the one from earlier?"

"Yeah. When both Selphy and Kuroka disappeared, she comforted me by teaching me to sing. That was the only time she ever did something for me without asking for any form of compensation."

If that was the case, then who exactly was that girl they just met?

She… seemed kind of lonely…

She was just like Zagan when Nephy first met him, just like Nephy herself when she decided to kill her emotions. And so, several days flowed by without them ever getting the chance to meet her again.

"I see. There's no method of dispelling my curse in Liucaon, huh?" Zagan's voice was unable to hide his disappointment. It had been four days since they came to the city at the bottom of the ocean, Atlastia. Currently, the elders of the races represented at the conference were gathered together in the guest room that was granted to Zagan's group. It was the very same room they had carried Lilith over to before. Lilith, who ended up spearheading the negotiations over the course of events, was kneeling down in the front with the elders of the sirens and succubi kneeling behind her. Behind them were Kuroka and Selphy. Zagan was reclining in a chair, and Nephy and Foll were standing by his sides.

The elders were reverently holding up a mirror and a jewel. Each were only big enough to fit snugly into one's hand. The mirror was the one Lilith had showed them the other day. They were the so-called Holy Treasures handed down in Liucaon, which meant all three of their Holy Treasures were assembled once you added in Kuroka's blades.

"These are the three Holy Treasures passed down among our people. We possess no means of dispelling a curse, but we do believe they may be of use to you, Lord Archdemon," the siren elder replied to Zagan as sweat ran down their brow.

"I don't need them. Such tools choose their owners. They won't reply to me even if you hand them over."

199

Besides, how do you plan on protecting yourselves if I take them with me? Letting go of their main defensive options would have been a huge mistake. Their Holy Treasures were similar to celestial mysticism. If it came to a fight, they could put outstanding power on display, but they also had other applications. Unfortunately, while it may have been possible to use one to prevent a curse, they weren't tools that could dispel one.

However, Zagan didn't feel he had the right to complain. He came to them looking for a possibility outside of sorcery because he couldn't do anything himself. And, as he let out a deep sigh, he realized that Lilith had turned completely pale.

Oh, that's no good. It must sound like I'm chastising them... Zagan cleared out his throat with a cough to prepare himself to speak.

"You have no need to worry. You've upheld your promise. I don't care if you use my name to protect your precious people. An Archdemon's sway will not waver due to some trivial change in form."

"Thank you... Also, I'm terribly sorry. We weren't very helpful," Lilith replied as she bowed down deeply.

"I'm telling you not to worry. More importantly, I'm a little tired. You may leave."

With that, the elders timidly left the room. And as they did, the siren elder called out to Selphy.

"Ainselph. You are an incompetent child who ran away from the royal family, but it is also true that you have the most talent for singing among all the princesses. You may keep this."

After saying that, the elder slapped a blue jewel into her hand.

"Huh... HUUUUUUH!? Isn't this, like, an heirloom?"

"Can't you at least call it a Holy Treasure...? This is about all we can offer the Archdemon. From now on, devote yourself to serving him."

200

"...Huh? Aren't I, like, being treated as a total accessory to the Holy Treasure here?"

The elder mercilessly chose not to deny that, which made Selphy let out a helpless laugh.

"Well, I wasn't, like, going to quit my job anyway, so I don't really mind..."

"Selphy. Mister looks pretty tired, so let's head out," Kuroka stated. Out of consideration for Zagan, the two of them lightly bowed before leaving the room. And after that, Foll also left Zagan's side.

"Foll, where are you going?" Zagan asked.

"...I want to get a look at the view," Foll replied. Her tone made it obvious that she felt responsible for their current situation.

It's not like it's your fault... This was brought about by Zagan's own carelessness, so there was no way he could resent her. However, Zagan knew his words would never get through to her, which meant his only option was to silently see her off.

In the end, the only ones left in the room were Zagan and Nephy. And, obviously, that meant the room was dead silent. Still, he was happy that Nephy was by his side.

However, before long, one of them decided to break the silence.

"Sorry, Nephy," Zagan apologized in a despondent tone.

"Why are you apologizing to me, Master Zagan?" Nephy asked as she stared back at him with wonder.

"Because we're at the bottom of the ocean. My sense of time is a little off... but today is the day I promised to go on a date with you."

And yet, Zagan was unable to return to his original form. He ended up breaking his promise in every conceivable way. But despite that, Nephy simply clasped her chest, then aimed a gentle smile at him.

"Please do not pay it any mind. I will wait as long it takes."

"It'll be another ten years before I grow back to my normal form…" Zagan mumbled. Though, it wasn't even clear if he was going to grow. And yet, Nephy just shook her head as if it were no big deal.

"I know. I will wait for ten or even a hundred years. After all, that much time is nothing to a sorcerer. Isn't that right, Master Zagan?"

No, I can't keep her waiting ten years… Back when Nephy was turned into a child, Zagan felt the same way, but he had something urgent he had to give her.

"Nephy, stoop down," Zagan stood up from his chair, then turned to face Nephy as he said that.

"Huh? Like this?"

Zagan pulled a pendant out from his pocket and placed it around her neck. It was the mithril pendant Orias left behind for her.

"Master Zagan, what is this…?" Nephy asked him that question as she stared at him in surprise.

"I found it in the hidden elven village. It was the one and only thing you had when you were brought to that village, Nephy," Zagan explained as he cast his gaze downward and clenched his jaw.

I wanted to end our date with this… However, there was no way he could make Nephy and Orias wait ten years. And so, as he looked down, he saw drops of water fall to the ground.

This is… the first time I've felt so pathetic… This was likely also the first time that he found himself unable to hold back his tears. And upon seeing Zagan like that, Nephy embraced him lovingly.

"Thank you very much… for giving me something so precious… Master Zagan," Nephy croaked out, then brought her cheek to his as if to comfort him and continued, "But it's fine. I know that you've been trying your best to protect us, so at least for this one moment, it's fine to let your guard down. Don't try to hide your emotions."

Her embrace was extremely tender as Zagan followed her invitation and buried his face in her chest.

It's so warm... And it was soft, too.

This was the first time Zagan had exposed his raw emotions since he had found someone he loved, since he had decided never to appear weak in order to protect his loved ones.

Clinging on to Nephy's body, he remained perfectly still without stirring until the tears that fell from his eyes dried up. In the end, neither of them knew how much time had passed. And when his tears finally stopped, Zagan embarrassingly sniffed up his mucus.

"Ummm... Sorry. I showed you... something embarrassing."

"There's nothing to be embarrassed about. Honestly, I'm happy you've shown me a new side of you."

I can never beat Nephy... Their roles were the exact opposite of how they usually were, but oddly enough, it didn't feel bad. No, on the contrary, it may have been like this from the very beginning. Nephy understood everything about Zagan, accepted it, and stayed by his side regardless, so hadn't she always been supporting him?

"Besides, I don't believe you will break your promise, Master Zagan?"

"Huh...? What do you mean?"

Right as he said that, a pain like his heart had just been pierced ran through his body, which made him collapse.

"Gaaaah!"

"Master Zagan!" Nephy screamed, but Zagan was unable to answer.

What is this pain? It was felt like mana was being sucked out of his heart. Sweat poured out his entire body, and he was unable to breathe. And then, the door to the room flew open without even a knock.

"Zagan, this is bad!"

It was Chastille, who was left completely speechless when she saw Zagan passed out in Nephy's arms.

"Chastille... You're right... This is bad... Master Zagan has collapsed..."

"Huh...? Is this related to the thing outside?" Chastille muttered that to herself as if she hadn't even heard Nephy's words.

"What do you mean? What happened outside?"

Finally returning to her senses, Chastille nodded quickly. Then, her face paled as she tried to form the right words.

"A monster's attacking... and it's just like the one Bifrons summoned... I think it may be the Demon Lord."

And so, the exact situation that Zagan feared most had just occurred. He was stuck in the body of a child, unable to use Heaven's Phosphor, when an unkillable enemy was preparing to slaughter all those around him.

A little while earlier, Foll aimlessly wandered out of the temple after leaving Zagan's room. She distanced herself from both the temple and the town and simply walked about at the bottom of the ocean. Lilith's song was fresh on her mind. The tale of her father was great, and she was happy to hear it, yet...

I'm... the bad dragon... She had cast a curse on Zagan, and unlike in the story, there was no way to dispel it. Even though she wished to be stronger in order to help him, she ended up doing the exact opposite. Zagan's expression when he heard that there was no way of dispelling the curse was burned into her eyes and wouldn't go away. He looked to be on the verge of tears.

"This isn't… how it was supposed to go…" Foll mumbled. She thought that if she were stronger, Zagan would be happy. However, the result was different. After her body grew bigger, her power also grew proportionally, but it still wasn't enough. She failed to destroy a member of the Night Clan, who was a being of lower rank than her. And despite everything, Zagan was still strong in his child form. He continued to not show his weakness and conducted himself with majesty.

The reason Foll didn't get stronger was because she was weak. Because she didn't understand something so simple, she couldn't accept it, and that brought misfortune to those around her. If that was not the act of a child, then what was it?

"What should I do now…?" Foll asked herself. Even after becoming smaller, even when he couldn't find a means of reversing his transformation, Zagan never once tried to blame Foll for it. And even if he yelled and cursed at her, he would surely comfort her pitiful self in the end.

Zagan would never do that… He watched over Foll in a kindly and strict manner. When she did something wrong, he would correct her. If she did something well, he would praise her. He'd only been by her side a few months, but the warmth she received from him was far greater than even what her Father had provided her in the past. That was why she was able to rely on him from the bottom of her heart. However, that was also painful at times, as he never once relied on her.

I wonder if Zagan is getting Nephy's help right now… Nephy was the only one capable of comforting Zagan. Foll was happy he had someone who he could lean on, but at the same time, she was sad she couldn't lend him her shoulder. All she could do was leave the two of them alone, which made her feel insignificant. She really hated herself. And, right as she sank to the floor in sorrow and hugged her knees, she heard a sweet voice.

"Heeheehee, oh dear, is the cute little fawn lost?"

"...Who's there?" Foll asked as she looked up again and spotted a 'shadow' lurking about in front of her eyes. Despite her enhanced draconic senses, she couldn't make out the figure clearly. And that had nothing to do with the poor visibility at the bottom of the ocean. No, she was simply unable to perceive it... It almost felt like its very existence was blurred, as if it didn't have a particular shape at all.

"Alshiera...?" Foll uttered the first name that came to mind. She thought the vampire had dodged her attack during their earlier clash, but that form made her doubt that. After all, it wouldn't have been all that strange for Alshiera to end up like that due to her draconic might.

The shadow then let out a curious laugh.

"What a naughty child. A naughty child who stole something important from that gentleman. Still, you're also a clever one who carried it all the way here... Eeheehee. Keeheehee. Ahahahahah," the shadow spat out some ominous words, then cackled wildly.

A mysterious sensation assaulted Foll as she raised her guard.

I have a bad feeling about this... Can I even hit her? If she unleashed her breath here, Atlastia would be reduced to rubble. On the other hand, she didn't think the sorcery she fired earlier would have any effect, so Foll prepared some sorcery to hold her back for the time being.

"I didn't... steal anything," Foll explained. And then, she held up her right hand, showing that she was ready to fire off sorcery at a moment's notice. However, a dark substance coiled around her arm as if to mock her vigilance.

"What a naughty fawn. It's not good to lie," the shadow replied. And in that instant, Foll saw them. She saw the golden eyes on the other side of the 'shadow' that seemed to be fading. And within those golden eyes, she saw pure, unfiltered hatred for anything and everything in the world.

"Don't touch me!" Foll exclaimed as she tried to shake off the black haze. However, her body froze.

I can't put more strength into my arm... Her hands were pitifully trembling, and even the strength in her knees gave out. For some reason, those golden eyes made the strength drain out of her body.

What is this? Sorcery? Foll didn't understand what was going on at all.

"Still, you may be at ease. All who inhabit this world are thieves. They betrayed him, gouged out his eyes, dug out his heart, severed his limbs, plucked off his head, and even stole all that remained of his corpse... They are criminals who torment him even now... Aaaaaaaaah, how repulsive. They should all just perish!"

What am I feeling right now...? Fear...? Am I... scared? Foll finally started to understand why she was losing strength upon seeing the insanity within those golden eyes. Even though she was young, she was a dragon, yet she was now feeling fear to such an extent that she lost her voice. Foll's body should have been bigger than the shadow, but she was trembling pathetically and even had tears spilling from her eyes. A red tongue peeked out from the shadow, then crawled across the back of Foll's right hand... where the sigil was.

"Ooh! Oooh! This pulsation! Welcome back, my beloved Master ********. I'll release you from there right this instant!"

Immediately following that, the shadow swelled up, then loomed over Foll's body.

No! I don't want this! Save me, Zagan! And the last sight Foll saw was...

"I won't let you!"

The figure of a girl who possessed the same golden eyes as the shadow.

"What... is this?" Zagan muttered. After leaving the temple, he caught sight of a squirming mass of meat and bones, which made him ask, "Are these entrails...?"

That was indeed what it resembled, but the problem was its size. The mass of meat was big enough to cover a large mass of land. It was still quite far away from the temple, but if it reached them, it could swallow the entire town. Where did something of that size come from? What did it want? Zagan had many questions, but knew nothing except the fact that if it moved toward them, everyone was doomed.

"It certainly does remind me of the Demon Lord," Nephy remarked. However, it was different from the sludge they found before. This time around, it had a clearly defined mass to it.

"Is that... alive?" Chastille asked as she pointed a trembling finger toward it. It was covered in countless veins that were pulsating in a creepy manner, numerous bones were sticking out of it to support its structure, and something akin to blood was dripping out from it.

It was alive. However, it was something so hideous that it didn't even resemble any creature above or within the ocean.

"Is that a cocoon?" Barbatos asked as he skulked out of Chastille's shadow with a grimace on his face.

"A cocoon?" Zagan replied as he cast his gaze over it once more. He had a point. It seemed to be encasing something, but Zagan didn't have the slightest idea what would hatch.

Chastille, the members of the church, Kuroka, Lilith, Selphy, and the elders were all gathered together with Zagan and Nephy.

"Angelic Knights, help evacuate the civilians and the guests. Kuroka, Nephteros, stay with me. We'll deal with..." Chastille raised her voice as she addressed her subordinates, but then trailed off. She'd lost her train of thought in the middle of speaking because she realized something was amiss. There were two people missing.

"...Hey, where are Foll and Nephteros?" Zagan inquired. He assumed they were nearby, but his adopted daughter and sister-in-law were nowhere in sight.

"Master Zagan, look!" Nephy exclaimed as she pointed at a single bat floating in the air. It seemed to be wounded, and was unsteadily fluttering toward them as if to escape the mass of meat before vanishing into the shadow of a rocky surface. Strengthening his vision using sorcery, Zagan spotted something that looked like a human hand.

"Tch, someone collapsed over there!" Zagan explained. The hand that he saw in the distance was thin and feminine. Zagan leaped down from the temple without hesitation, and ran over to the rocky area where the bat vanished.

"Nephteros?" Zagan called out his sister-in-law's name, since she was the one who had collapsed there. Perhaps because she was fighting with that mass of meat, she had wounds all over her body.

"Ugh..." Nephteros opened her golden eyes with a groan.

"Nephteros, what happened?"

"Big Bro…?" Nephteros said as she shook her head and got up. Apparently her wounds weren't all that deep. And by that point, Nephy also caught up with them.

"Are you alright? I'll heal you…"

"Heal…? Oh, I'm fine! More importantly, what about Foll!?"

Zagan and Nephy exchanged glances.

"What do you mean? Were you with Foll?"

"That child was attacked by something…" Nephteros began muttering as she searched through her memories.

"By something, you mean that monster?" Zagan asked.

"No, that's wrong. This is just a guess… but I think it was Alshiera," Nephteros replied upon having the mountain of meat pointed out to her.

"Just a guess? You didn't see her face or anything?"

"She was covered by a sort of black fog. I couldn't really tell," Nephteros said as she grabbed her shoulders and began trembling as she drew back as if trying to get away from the mass of meat. Then, she continued, "I had the same sense of discomfort when I was swallowed by the Demon Lord. I tried to save Foll… but she couldn't be…" Nephteros trailed off as she lost consciousness.

Zagan's heart started to pound out of worry for his daughter. And, as he stared at his enemy, several bats wrapped around the mountain of meat. It looked like they were sinking their fangs into it as the bats tore several chunks of it away, which revealed Foll wrapped in what appeared to be a rib.

"Foll!" Zagan screamed. She was far enough away that his voice wouldn't reach her, but Foll faintly opened her eyes, looked at him, and moved her lips.

S A V E M E

Zagan could definitely tell that was what she was trying to say. However, at that exact moment, the mass of meat began moving as if it had just woken up.

"Barbatos! Take Chastille along and save Foll!" Zagan slammed his fist into the ground as he barked out those commands. Even in his weakened state, a small fissure formed in the bedrock at the bottom of the ocean. And in response, the shadow at his feet wriggled.

"... Tch, fine. You ready, crybaby?"

"Don't call me crybaby. If I don't put in some work at times like this, I'll never finish repaying my debt."

Crossing over the shadows, Chastille and Barbatos emerged directly above where Foll was trapped.

"Shine — Sacred Sword Azrael!" Chastille roared as her Sacred Sword cast a light and tore apart the bone and meat surrounding Foll's body.

"Now Barbatos!"

Foll's body was now detached from the meat, so Barbatos stretched out his hand, but...

"Whoa, the hell!?"

An enormous claw pierced the meat, which made Barbatos take evasive action.

Huh? It changed form...? Left with no foothold, Chastille began descending the mountain of flesh.

"Chastille! Don't fucking touch it! This is bad!" Barbatos exclaimed. However, Chastille wasn't a sorcerer. Plus, they were at the bottom of the ocean, so she had no means of preventing her descent... Luckily, Zagan didn't throw them in without a plan.

"Master Zagan, that's..." Nephy gulped as she noticed the irregularity. The fissure that Zagan formed with his fist began stretching out and chased after Barbatos and Chastille as if it had a will of its own. Looking at it again, it seemed to almost look like a massive magic circle.

"Heaven's Scale Snowfield," Zagan called out that name, and the magic circle engraved at the bottom of the ocean began shining as countless lights appeared around the mountain of meat.

In my current form, I need an enormous magic circle to perform any sorcery... What a bother... This was the Snowfield that Zagan improved using Nephy's advice. And if not for her input, he wouldn't have been able to activate it as he was now. Zagan extended his snowfield to run beneath Chastille's feet and caught her right before she touched that ominous mound.

"We're falling back, Chastille," Barbatos stated as he picked up Chastille, passed through the shadows, and appeared next to Zagan. However, in that mere instant, the mass of meat finished its transformation. And Zagan's group was left completely speechless upon witnessing its completed form.

It had wings large enough that it felt like they covered the skies, jaws big enough that it looked like it could swallow houses whole, fangs peeking up from under its lips, and was covered in black scales. A black dragon.

"Black Dragon Marbas...?" Nephy muttered like she couldn't believe her eyes, but Zagan had never heard that name before.

"What's that?"

"Miss Lilith just told us a story about it. Marbas is a dragon in Liucaon's legends that Foll's father defeated..." Nephy muttered. That was confusing. Why did the monster who swallowed Foll take that form?

No, that's not it... Zagan rose his hand to his chest upon realizing the painful truth.

"That's just Foll's current dragon form. The blackness is likely my... or rather, the Sigil of the Archdemon's color. It mixed with Foll's power and took on that shape."

"Then, you're saying that's also an extension of your curse?" Nephteros asked, gulping audibly as she heard his explanation.

"...We've been trying to keep the flow of power balanced this whole time, so something must have tipped the scales," Zagan stated. This definitely wasn't a natural occurrence. Something out there caused this.

Hm, is that thing different from the Demon Lord...? When he first saw it, he felt it was the same as the Demon Lord he fought on the boat. However, once it gained a form, it seemed far too different. There was also the possibility that Orobas fought something other than the Demon Lord in Raphael's dreams. After all, none of them knew anything about the Demon Lord in the first place...

None of that matters now! Zagan shook his thoughts off and glared at the black dragon.

"I'll have you return my daughter!" Zagan proclaimed. And then, the lights of the Snowfield converged onto a single point. This sorcery wasn't completely developed. It was still just a stepping stone toward his true goal.

Take a good look, Foll. This is the power I meant to grant you! Zagan wove together something he designed for Foll alone.

"Heaven's Scale Dragon Form!"

The lights suddenly took on the shape of a golden dragon. It seemed the thousands of lights that made up the snowfield were merely components that made up the Dragon Form. He was certain it would ensure his victory, but then something odd happened.

213

"Huh…?" Zagan mumbled as his eyes, ears, nose, and mouth all boiled over with blood.

"Master Zagan!" Nephy screamed as he collapsed to his knees without even understanding just what had happened. And after being caught by Nephy, he couldn't even move a single finger.

"Hey, Zagan! What's going on!? The hell'd that monster do!?" Barbatos exclaimed, demanding answers.

"…You've got it all wrong. The number of circuits he constructed surpassed his limit… This is what happens when you use sorcery after exhausting all your mana," Nephteros responded. It had only been half a month since Nephteros was left on the verge of death due to her overuse of sorcery. And precisely because of that, her judgment was swift.

"Nephelia, treat him now! Your mysticism can handle it, right?"

"Okay!" Nephy replied as she embraced Zagan and closed her eyes to offer a prayer. And, as she did, her body glowed faintly and the pain building up in Zagan's body lightened. This wasn't sorcery, but mysticism.

I'm holding everyone back right now… Zagan wanted to lament his powerlessness, but found himself unable to even speak. He was falling into despair over being able to do nothing when his precious daughter was in mortal danger.

"Chastille, you take the front. I'll amplify your Sacred Sword with my celestial mysticism," Nephteros ordered as she started taking command of the situation.

"The technique that brought down the chimera, huh...? Are you certain it'll work against a dragon?" Chastille asked. Though, honestly, they didn't have any other options.

I shouldn't have left Gremory and Kimaris behind... They were the only two people Zagan had taught Heaven's Phosphor to.

No, Foll would get caught up in Heaven's Phosphor anyway... In any case, they were the only people not present that he could've relied on.

"[Thou art he who rules over terror. Accompanied by the god of war, become he who brings about—!]" Nephteros began chanting her celestial mysticism, but the black dragon interrupted her by flapping its wings. And that single flap turned the ocean currents into a whirlpool, causing a vortex of destruction that reduced even the huge rocks at the bottom of the sea to dust. That scene was just like...

"A tsunami inside the ocean...?" someone muttered in a trembling frightened tone. And, judging that her celestial mysticism wouldn't cut it, Nephteros searched for other possible solutions.

"Barbatos!"

"It's no good. Didn't I say I can't use the shadows well here!?"

The Holy Treasure of the sirens that protected their city obstructed sorcerers, preventing them from fully manifesting their power. That was why Zagan crumbled to the ground and couldn't invoke his sorcery... It seemed they had no means of escaping the black dragon's tsunami.

This is my fault... I never should've relied on them... They were all going to die because Zagan asked them for their help. If he had never done that, they would have been safe and sound. And, just as Zagan was overwhelmed by his own sense of powerlessness...

"Neptunia's Ainselph so sings. Hear me, Holy Treasure, Neptune's Tear!"

A dignified voice suddenly rang out of nowhere, followed by a melody with no words.

Is this... Selphy? Right when Zagan realized that, a whirling tide rose before the black dragon. And, as the slender whirlpool coiled around it like a tornado, the black dragon's tsunami dissipated. However, it simply opened its jaws and began gathering mana in response.

Is it planning on unleashing its breath!? If it combined Foll's mana with that of the Sigil of the Archdemon, then the entire town would be annihilated. Having failed to construct the Dragon Form, Zagan possessed no means of blocking it. Or at least, that should have been the case, but...

"I won't let you do as you please in someone else's home!"

The next one to fly out of the temple was Lilith, who had the mirror they were shown before in her hands. It was likely quite firm as a shield, but it was far too small to stop the breath of a dragon. However, in an unexpected turn, the light from the mirror spread out.

"In the name of the Silver-Eyed King, demonstrate your power. Holy Treasure, Hades' Mirror!"

The light spread out as if to cover the entire temple, then transformed into something akin to an enormous crest in a magic circle. The black dragon's breath collided with it, breaking through it slowly. And yet, Lilith had a confident smile on her face.

217

"Have a taste of your own medicine!"

Immediately following that, a crest of light spread out directly above the black dragon, and a mass of mana descended down upon it.

It bent space and sent the breath back at it? Zagan finally understood why Lilith's Holy Treasure looked like a mirror. Mirrors reflected light, much like how their Holy Treasure could distort mana and any physical substances.

And as the black dragon's posture collapsed, Kuroka took the lead.

"Here we go... Moonless Sky!"

Kuroka's paired sword seemingly resonated with the other two Holy Treasures. Light stretched out from them toward the heavens, like towers, and she swung them down right at the dragon's neck.

"HAAAAAA!" Kuroka let out a yell, and her blades easily tore through the black scales, sending blackened blood bursting out. However, the one wielding those blades was Kuroka, who would never stop at a thin cut to the skin. And so, she moved to strike at its torso, then its neck. Without letting her swords' momentum slow, she twisted her blade from its throat to its body, and unleashed a barrage of continuous strikes.

The miracle brought about by her twin swords of light resembled an enormous blooming flower. And before long, when Kuroka's swords came to a stop, the black dragon collapsed to the ground with a thud.

These are Liucaon's Holy Treasures... Upon witnessing the destructive power of Kuroka's twin blades, Zagan felt that there may have been something in these lands that strengthened the power of the Holy Treasures. Or perhaps they were just stronger when used together. Whatever the case, they seemed to be far more powerful than Chastille or Raphael's Sacred Swords.

"Please take a rest, Mister. It looks like I can finally pay you back here," Kuroka said as she lifted up her swords with a smile on her face.

"Yeah! I'll, like, totally give it my all too! We can't, like, have Mister Zagan do all the heavy lifting in our home!" Selphy added. Then, she pushed Lilith's back and continued, "Come on, you too Lilith."

"Huh? Um, I'm not trying to make up for failing to fulfill my promise or anything, but I'll properly pay back the debt we owe you for lending us your power."

With that, the three girls went on to challenge the black dragon.

"Come on, we have to help them. You aren't just going to let a bunch of amateurs face that thing alone, are you?" Nephteros asked as she stood up and stuck her hand out to Chastille.

"I get it. You'll accompany us, won't you, Barbatos?"

"…Fine."

The three of them joined in on the battle as well.

They're all fighting, so why am I moping around? His daughter was begging for his help, but he couldn't answer her hopes and was even clinging to his bride for comfort.

What the hell kind of parent am I!? Unfortunately, Zagan's body had been torn to shreds already, so any attempt to move was in vain. His mana was flowing wildly in random directions, and even breathing sent pain shooting through his body to the point where he felt ready to faint. However, he couldn't just remain in such a pathetic state.

"I'm... alright, Nephy... Go help them..." Zagan mumbled. There was more mana flowing at the bottom of the ocean than above land, which meant the power of spirits Nephy used was bound to be more effective. He was sure that her power would be more useful when it came to saving Foll, but Nephy embraced Zagan and wouldn't let him go.

"...Master Zagan, I'm sorry," Nephy replied in a regretful voice, then added, "To be honest, I thought it would be fine if your curse wasn't dispelled."

Nephy made that confession as if she had betrayed him.

"Nephy..."

However, Zagan found himself unable to blame her for those feelings.

"When you were turned into a child... I thought the exact same thing."

At that time, Nephy was an innocent child who could naturally smile. She had no painful memories, and had a blindingly brilliant future ahead of her. It should have been possible for Nephy to grow up just like that, having cast aside all her painful memories.

But I like Nephy as she is now... Zagan fell in love with the Nephy who was born as a result of those painful memories. That was why he dragged Orias out and returned Nephy to normal.

"But it's different, right? Thinking that you should stay as you are is the same as denying all that time you've spent doing your best to live, right?" Nephy gazed right into Zagan's eyes as she said that, then continued, "I'm not a pure maiden like in those stories. I've done horrible things, and imagined even worse, but... even so, I want to be of use to you, Master Zagan. Will you accept me?"

Zagan's consciousness was growing hazy, so he was unable to discern the true meaning behind Nephy's words. Still, he smiled as widely as he could.

"Isn't it obvious… that I'll accept you? Haven't you… done the same for me… this whole time?"

Even when Zagan was degraded to such a powerless state, there was no way he wouldn't accept Nephy. And upon hearing that reply, Nephy let out a deep, heartfelt sigh.

"Then… please accept this. This is… all that I can offer you."

Nephy placed her lips atop Zagan's.

Huuuuuuuuuuuuuuh!? What!? Why are we kissing now!?

That was something Zagan planned to initiate himself… not that it really mattered… Zagan's eyes darted about in complete confusion as he experienced his first kiss. However, at the same time, he felt the flow of mana in his body return to normal.

A path opened…? The newly opened path ran through Zagan and repaired the broken flow within his body. And not just the backlash from using Dragon Form, either. It even repaired the flow from the Sigil of the Archdemon.

At that moment, he was reminded of a fairy tale he heard during his days as a waif. He forgot the exact details, but the only thing that was able to return the cursed prince to normal… was a kiss from the princess… And, as if to recount that fairy tale, his small body began to change.

His thin and unreliable arms turned thick and sturdy. His short legs were now firmly planted on the ground. He had to look up at Nephy before, but now he was tall enough to look down at her. His clothes changed, transforming into his usual robes like he had set up beforehand. And, by the time his lips parted from Nephy's due to his growth, Zagan's body had completely returned to its usual form, which left even Nephy, who kissed him in the first place, staring at him in shock.

"Y-You really... returned to... normal?" Nephy asked.

"Y-Yeah. Looks like..." Zagan replied, unable to even believe their good fortune.

"Did you know about this, Nephy? That a curse can be broken like that, I mean."

"W-Well, there was a scene like that in a story I heard recently..." Nephy's ears turned red as she mumbled those words before she continued with, "But... it was something Miss Lilith said she learned from Miss Alshiera, so I thought it might be related..."

It was a hint from Alshiera...? Even though she seemed to be provoking, making fun of, and messing with Zagan, she indirectly gave Nephy advice on what to do. Thinking back on it, he realized she was likely also the one who showed them where Nephteros and Foll were earlier. However, it also looked like she was the who attacked Foll in the first place... What were her true intentions?

"She doesn't matter right now. I need to save our troublesome daughter," Zagan stated with a shake of his head. Then, he held his hand out to the sky, where the scattered lights of the Snowfield still remained. His sorcery was still in effect. That was why he was confident he could show them its true form at last.

"Heaven's Scale Dragon Form."

The lights of the Snowfield gathered once more at his call, and this time they took on the form he intended. Suddenly, a golem that possessed a dragon's form was kneeling before them.

"Let's go, Nephy. We're going to get Foll back."

"Yes, Master Zagan!"

And just like that, the two of them headed off to do battle with the black dragon.

When Zagan and Nephy charged in atop the Dragon Form, the black dragon unleashed its breath at them without any hesitation. Lilith deployed her Holy Treasure to try and block the attack, but Zagan was just a little too far away for her to make it.

"It's no good!" Lilith yelled out in despair. But Zagan simply replied with a haughty laugh.

"Don't waver! The Archdemon you serve yields to no one!" Zagan roared as his golem crashed into the black dragon's breath and swallowed every last ounce of its mana. Immediately after that, the black dragon flapped its wings to flee upward.

"Nope! You won't get away!" Selphy exclaimed as she held out her jewel and manipulated the ocean's currents, obstructing the black dragon's movements. Thanks to that, it could no longer flap its wings, so it was stuck. And so, since both its breath and wings were sealed, it tried to use its claws to strike down the Dragon Form, but...

"I won't let you!"

"Go, Zagan!"

Kuroka and Chastille used their blades to sever the black dragon's forefeet. Then, Barbatos used the shadows to pull them away to a safe distance, since they had left themselves utterly defenseless.

At that point, there was nothing left to obstruct him, so Zagan landed on the black dragon. And when he did, he spotted Foll buried within its head. She was still bigger than she originally was, but it was clear she'd begun to return to her original form.

"I'm here to pick you up, Foll."

"Zagan…?" Foll dimly opened her eyes, looked up at him, and mumbled his name upon hearing his declaration.

"Just hold on. I'll clear away that nuisance," Zagan stated as he snapped his fingers, which made black sparks burst out all around Foll. It was a heavily suppressed Heaven's Phosphor. A large hole was formed in the black dragon's head, and all that was left was the young dragon. Then, as the two of them fell from the sky, Zagan gently embraced her. Foll probably had much she wanted to say and ask, but she couldn't manage to do much more than feebly cling to Zagan's chest. And as she did, Zagan and Nephy embraced their daughter together.

Glad I made it in time… Kuroka, Chastille, and the others may have been able to defeat the black dragon, but there was no guarantee they could have saved Foll. Zagan had nearly lost his precious daughter there.

"Seriously… don't make me worry so much."

The black dragon was still squirming around beneath them. Despite losing its core, it still seemed to possess some form of sentience. They were in a situation where it could bare its fangs upon them at any moment, but Zagan simply embraced Foll and brushed her head gently. And then, in a completely obvious turn of events, the black dragon opened its massive jaws and came rushing in.

"Za…gan… behind…" Foll called out to him in a faint voice, but Zagan didn't turn to look at the black dragon.

"It's alright, Foll. Master Zagan is here." Nephy said, acting as if she understood her role perfectly as she pressed her forehead against Foll's to calm her down. At that, Zagan stopped brushing his daughter's head, and lightly swung his hand toward the black dragon to drive it away. However, he wasn't clenching his fist, so it was like a casual wave to an acquaintance... Luckily, the Dragon Form was there to answer his greeting. Its golden tail smashed the black dragon's nose, making it shatter.

"Huh!?" Foll's eyes shot open in shock.

...*Hm? Its power has gone up quite a bit...* Naturally, he had meant for it to be quite powerful, but it still shouldn't have been strong enough to obliterate the black dragon's head. He pondered the matter, and a sudden thought came to mind. Perhaps it had grown because of the path that had been opened between him and Nephy... Whatever the case, the black dragon had become quiet, so Zagan finally let Foll go and looked at her face.

"You'll do well to remember this, Foll. Power isn't something that's simply used for destruction. It's something that can be stolen and gained from others."

"St...olen...?" Foll repeated his words, searching for the meaning behind them. And, after leaving his daughter to Nephy, Zagan had the Dragon Form ascend overhead. Having lost its core and its head, the black dragon was crumbling away.

But it's still kicking... Though it could no longer move, it was still a swelling mass of mana born from stealing the powers of a dragon and an Archdemon.

"Foll, you're a dragon. Dragons reign at the peak of all living beings, and are the world's strongest predators."

In the simplest of terms, they lived in a different realm from beings who had to consume food to live. Dragons pillaged and preyed upon power itself. He hoped she understood his point.

"Devour — Dragon Form."

The golem opened its jaws and engulfed the corpse of the black dragon. This was Heaven's Scale, a sorcery that devoured the mana of everything it touched and used it to amplify its own abilities. It didn't vanish instantly like Heaven's Phosphor, so in a way, it could be considered even more dangerous.

I modeled it after the dragons in legends... By that point, the black dragon couldn't maintain its form. And before long, the black dragon's body vanished into the dew, leaving absolutely nothing behind.

"I'm sorry, Zagan," Foll croaked out. She was a fair bit weaker now, since her body was back to normal. However, her rough breathing made it clear that wasn't the only issue, which was why Zagan was treating her with the mana he absorbed through the Dragon Form. Thanks to the precautions Zagan took earlier, her clothes had morphed back to the native dress she usually wore.

"I'm going to... get stronger in a way... that better matches my size..."

"Sounds good," Zagan brushed his daughter's head as he gave her that reply.

"The Dragon Form isn't vanishing..." Foll muttered as she cast her gaze through the window and spotted the golem standing guard outside.

"Yeah. It devoured a lot of mana this time, so it will probably stick around for quite some time."

In fact, it had gathered so much that it could fight on equal ground with an Archdemon for several years. The powers of a dragon and the Sigil of the Archdemon were terrifying enough on their own, but when combined, they were practically invincible.

A shield that eats away at its enemies and grows with time... Something that powerful could be considered the ultimate form of sorcery. Though, at the same time, only beings on par with Archdemons or dragons could ever hope to use it.

"I'm thinking of leaving it here. I told Lilith she's under my protection, so I need some way to guard her home."

The calamity that once threatened the city at the bottom of the ocean had become its defender. The elders were frightened by the idea, but they didn't shoot it down.

"Zagan, you're different from the Silver-Eyed King," Foll muttered in relief.

"What do you mean?"

"In the legend, the Silver-Eyed King couldn't save one of his dragon friends, so he had to kill them. But… you saved both and basically turned your enemy into an ally. You're way more amazing than him."

"In that case, I'm sure you'll grow to be far more amazing than him as well. You're my daughter, after all."

"Mm. I'll do my best," Foll replied as she nodded in satisfaction.

"Though, for now, you need to focus on resting. It'll help you heal faster."

"Okay… I'll do my best!"

Foll's stamina hadn't really returned, so she fell back asleep almost instantly after Zagan left her side.

Zagan found Nephy waiting for him outside Foll's room.

"How is she doing?"

"She seems fine. Your healing did the trick, Nephy."

Foll's life was still in danger after Zagan rescued her. The lingering mana from the sigil was too much for her younger body to handle. Luckily, Nephy managed to use it all to heal Foll. However, she didn't seem fully satisfied by that conclusion… Perhaps because she was confused by all the unexpected occurrences, including how the curse was dispelled.

"It seems there's something on your mind…" Zagan probed for more information as he folded his arms in front of his chest.

"Yes… Um, I can't help but wonder how the curse was dispelled," Nephy replied. She hadn't forgotten the kiss they shared, but she couldn't understand why it worked, which was why she worked up the courage to question him despite.

"Let's see… Well, if all we did was connect, um… a path between us, Foll and I wouldn't have regained our original forms."

If it was that simple, Zagan would have solved the issue right away. Or well, however long it took him to work up the courage to kiss her, anyway.

"It only worked because of the specific situation. We're lucky we had trustworthy allies around."

"What do you mean?"

"That black dragon was formed out of a mix of Foll's draconic powers and the Sigil of the Archdemon. In other words, it was a physical manifestation of the curse."

"I see. Basically, the curse sprang to life."

"That's what I think."

"It became a black dragon, then got injured by the Holy Treasures and a Sacred Sword. And in the end, you normalized the flow of my mana by forming a path between us. The curse was only dispelled because all three of those conditions were met."

It was the same for Chastille and the others. They only managed to wound the black dragon when the Holy Treasures and her Sacred Sword were working in tandem. If even one of them were missing, even Barbatos, though Zagan was reluctant to admit it, they likely would have been slaughtered.

In short, Zagan was saved by all the people he'd befriended thanks to Nephy.

Is this what it means to rely on others? It honestly doesn't feel too bad... Still, I need to finish off the person who dared to make Foll suffer... According to Nephteros, that was Alshiera.

"We must give our thanks to Miss Alshiera," Nephy said, her ears quivering about happily.

"Huh? Why? She may be the one who put Foll through all that."

"I know. I heard what Nephteros said, but considering everything that happened, doesn't it seem like she planned all this? I mean, the bats who showed us where Nephteros was were hers, right? And all of this ended with the curse on you getting dispelled..."

I feel like you're being far too kind to her... Zagan truly felt that way, but when he heard Nephy say that, he started to believe she was right. After all, the bats did guide Zagan's group.

"Well, let's just put her case on hold for now. It's not like we know where she is, anyway," Zagan said as he shook his head to free himself of such thoughts. It was possible she wasn't their enemy, but he didn't think she was an ally either. And so, he resolved to be better prepared for their next meeting.

Well, whatever. There's something more important on my mind right now... The curse may have been dispelled, but there was no way to regain the time he'd lost.

"Um... In the end, I wasn't able to keep my promise about our date, so why don't we resche—"

"No, you did not break your promise at all, Master Zagan," Nephy cut in, stopping his apology.

"Huh? No, I mean..." Zagan trailed off, unsure of how to respond.

"We went somewhere new, dressed up, and… did something special," Nephy replied as if reminiscing over happy memories. Then, she touched her own lips as her ears quivered about.

Oh, right! It did end with a kiss… Zagan recalled the moment, which made him turn even more red than Nephy.

"We managed to do everything you planned for our 'date,' Master Zagan."

"Maybe, but shouldn't we have done all that alone?"

"Didn't we spend a lot of time by ourselves?"

Zagan's memory of clinging to Nephy and crying in her arms sprung to mind when he heard that.

When she puts it like that, it does kind of feel like we went on a date…

"You're right. This may have been a date," Zagan said and he reached in and held Nephy's hand.

"I'm glad you agree," Nephy replied as she affectionately squeezed his hand back.

"So, when should our next date be?"

"…Excuse me?"

"It isn't like we're limited to one date! A lot of things went wrong, since this was our first attempt, so we have much to improve!"

"Well…" Nephy mumbled as she flashed an embarrassed smile. Then, in an unusual turn, she wrapped her arm around Zagan's and said, "I shall accompany you anywhere, Master Zagan."

On a later date, Gremory kicked up a huge fuss out of a desire to hear more about their date, but that is a story for another day.